Millionaire Mind Hacks

15 Steps to Igniting Your Inner Drive for Greatness

Abbix Publishing Company

© Copyright 2023 by Abbix Publishing Company- All rights reserved.

The content contained within this book may not be reproduced, duplicated or transmitted without direct written permission from the author or the publisher.

Under no circumstances will any blame or legal responsibility be held against the publisher, or author, for any damages, reparation, or monetary loss due to the information contained within this book, either directly or indirectly.

Legal Notice:

This book is copyright protected. It is only for personal use. You cannot amend, distribute, sell, use, quote or paraphrase any part, or the content within this book, without the consent of the author or publisher.

Disclaimer Notice:

Please note the information contained within this document is for educational and entertainment purposes only. All effort has been executed to present accurate, up to date, reliable, complete information. No warranties of any kind are declared or implied. Readers acknowledge that the author is not engaging in the rendering of legal, financial, medical or professional advice. The content within this book has been derived from various sources. Please consult a licensed professional before attempting any techniques outlined in this book.

By reading this document, the reader agrees that under no circumstances is the author responsible for any losses, direct or indirect, that are incurred as a result of the use of information contained within this document, including, but not limited to, errors, omissions, or inaccuracies.

Contents

Introduction	1
1. Chapter 1 - The Power of Positive Thinking: Unleashing Your Inner Optimist	5
Chapter 2 - Cultivating the Soil for Growth: The Power of a Growth Mindset	15
Chapter 3 - Breaking Down Negativity's Walls	24
2. Chapter 4 - Picturing Prosperity: The Power of Visualization	33
3. Chapter 5 - Creating Your Reality. The Law of Attraction and Positive Thinking	40
4. Chapter 6 - The Power of Positive Affirmations	49
5. Chapter 7 - Charting Your Financial Freedom Path	57
6. Chapter 8 - Charting Your Career Course with Positivity	65
7. Chapter 9 - Planting Positivity Seeds in Your Relationships	74
8. Chapter 10 - Invigorating Wellness. Positive Thinking for a Healthier You	81

Chapter 11 - Navigating Roadblocks on the Road to Positivity		91
9.	Chapter 12 - Fueling Your Journey with Unwavering Motivation	100
10.	Chapter 13 - Navigating the Sea of Skepticism	106
11.	Chapter 14 - Planting Positivity: Cultivating the Habit of Positive Thinking	115
Chapter 15 - Embracing Your Future with Positivity		121
Conclusion		128

Introduction

We live two parallel lives: the one in which we truly live and the one that lies unlived within us. Between the two stands negativity.

Have you ever stopped reading a book after the first few sentences? Have you ever ignored a call to start a spiritual practice or devote your life to helping others? Have you ever glimpsed a future of accomplishment, a journey to success, only to let it slip through your grasp? Have you ever wished you could become a mentor, an innovator, a supporter of the underprivileged and voiceless, run for government, fight for the environment, promote peace in the world, or protect the environment?

In the middle of the night, have you ever had a vision of the person you could become, the work you could accomplish, or the person you were meant to be?

Are you a musician who never composes music, a leader who never inspires their team or an entrepreneur who never started a business? Then you know what negativity is.

We unconsciously allow the negative forces of the mind to pass through the door of our hearts. We allow them in the space of who we are, allow them to take us over. These dark forces of mind interrupt the flow of life force and inhibit us from seeing beyond our limitations, stretching beyond our comfort zones, and reaching beyond ourselves. They make us focus on the negative, wallow in the negative, and obsess about the negative. They feed our fear, our despair, guilt, and hopelessness and steal our sense of safety, well-being, and peace. Like creeping shadows residing in the corners of our minds, they fuel attitudes that are damaging to our lives.

When mind monsters like negative emotions and thoughts become the dominating forces of our mind, we feel trapped in a never-ending vicious cycle that threatens to snuff out our very existence. Negative thoughts breed more negative thoughts and attract others, like forces, to them. When we let negative thoughts go unchecked in our minds, we hang a sign in the invisible world that will attract negative events, just as surely as the vultures are attracted to the carrion.

Hundreds of thousands, if not millions, of individuals, are yearning to conquer their negativity, cultivate a positive mindset, and live a life that allows them to develop and satisfy themselves. They are yearning to discover their true confidence, realize their genuine value, and grasp their mighty goal of soaring to greater heights. They are yearning to forge a novel path toward financial freedom in which they may live in joy, serenity, and optimism regardless of life's erratic gifts. They have shattered hearts and broken hopes. They are sick and tired of running on the never-ending treadmill of life with no end in sight.

If you're one of those warriors who is struggling to get out of the grip of negativity and limiting beliefs that hinder your pursuit of financial success, happiness, or reaching your life goals, then this book is for you.

This book covers fifteen steps to develop a positive mindset and reach your full potential. It will show you how to break free from the barriers that hinder your path to greatness and financial success.

As you read through this book, you'll gain a sound understanding of how to develop a growth mindset. When you have a growth mindset, you embrace challenges and setbacks as opportunities for learning and growth. You view failures as stepping stones toward improvement.

This book tells a lot about overcoming a negative mindset. It explains how to reprogram your mind to develop positivity and stay consistent on your journey.

This book also explains how to leverage the Law of Attraction for prosperity.

When you gain mastery over this powerful law, you'll be able to turn your intentions into reality, although it takes serious willpower, patience, and persistence.

You're an incredible powerhouse capable of transforming your thought energy into the physical forms of your choosing. No matter how big, small, or challenging it may seem, you can bring it into existence with your positive energy and intention.

You have come to this earth for a definite purpose. Nature has given you all the gifts, and abilities you need to fulfill this purpose. You have a well of potential within yourself. But you have to do your part by starting to tap into it. This book will provide you with the tools to do it.

In this book, you'll also learn techniques to foster positivity in relationships and enhance wellness. When you have a positive mental and emotional state, you feel secure and worthwhile. You enjoy a sense of confidence and feel in control of your life. A healthy emotional state enables you to break free from the traditional mold and be truly yourself. You flow with the stream of life and live effortlessly. You find optimistic ways of dealing with difficulties and conquering challenges without exerting negative force.

As you go through the book, you may find yourself challenged by some ideas that I employ and invite you to embrace. If it happens, I recommend that you remain open-minded and experiment with those ideas. I may also make some claims in this book that sound hard to believe. If these moments occur for you, I ask you to bear with me and give my ideas a try. When you see the result, you'll be convinced on your own.

Chapter One

Chapter 1 - The Power of Positive Thinking: Unleashing Your Inner Optimist

The Essence of Positive Thinking

Do you think highly of yourself? Do you have a constructive and helpful way of thinking? Do you focus on the silver lining, or do you concentrate on the negative aspects? Do you think in terms of winning and achieving success?

Positive thinkers see themselves as nice, loving people who deserve the nice things that life has to offer. They look for the best in themselves, others, and the world at large. They zero in on potential means of action and implement them. They have a "can do" and "will do" approach to life, always optimistic that success will bloom where effort is put in.

Take Emma, a positive thinker. As an ambitious actress in her early forties, Emma thought that her age would benefit her, not hold her back. She dedicated herself to honing her acting skills by taking acting lessons from renowned teachers. She started each day with a positive mindset and attended auditions whenever possible. Each audition gave Emma the chance to showcase her skills.

She was confident that her acting career would eventually blossom, so she persevered through countless temporary disappointments and improved her acting confidence. One day, she received an offer for a key role in a big-budget movie. She was so good in the part that it helped her achieve popularity as an actress.

The amazing thing about positive thinking is that it can be used right now or at any point in the future. You may simply make the quantum jump from negative to positive thinking!

Imagine that you and a friend have made plans to meet for dinner at a typical restaurant. You're wearing normal casual clothing. The restaurant is not very appealing, but it offers some level of coziness in its seating arrangements. The food is not very exceptional; there is nothing special about it. The music in the background is okay. Your friend is a negative person who tends to focus on the bad aspects of things.

Most of the evening is spent with her discussing her husband. She complains to you that he is making her life difficult and that she can't take it any longer. She even made some funny jokes about him. You take in what she has to say and acknowledge that he is a jerk. You make no effort to locate a remedy for the problem. Here is part of the conversation:

The negative person: My husband is bringing me down. Even when he is being kind to me, he is emotionally abusive. I'm exhausted from having to avoid offending him at all costs.

Negative you: He's a jerk. Why do you continue to tolerate him?

Negative person: I worry that I won't be able to find somebody more suitable, and I don't have much hope that I will.

Negative you: If that's how you feel, then I suppose you'll just have to grit your teeth and suffer for a little longer.

How do the two of you now feel?

Now picture yourself as a positive person. You decide to make plans to have dinner with the same friend at your preferred restaurant. You look perfect. The atmosphere is perfect, and the chairs are soft and supportive. You both concur that the food is excellent.

The in-house pianist can even perform some of your favorites. Your friend tells you about her troubles. You steer the conversation toward finding the best way to solve the problem. You help your friend play up her strengths and work around her flaws so that she may make the most of her chances. You concentrate on her finest qualities, favorite activities, and the most effective means of attaining her vital objectives. You encourage her to be her best! Let's listen in on a part of the talk:

Negative Person: My husband really makes me feel bad. He sometimes does nice things for me, but he hurts me deeply. I'm sick of having to constantly watch my steps around him.

Positive You: It seems like things are tough for you right now. I'd like to ask you three things. Why do you allow his inappropriate behavior? What choices do you have? What do you believe is the most effective solution?

Negative Person: I'm afraid of losing him and of being by myself. I have three choices, I suppose. I can tolerate his bad behavior, confront him, or leave. I need to get over my fear of being alone to show him that I won't put up with his rudeness.

Positive You: That makes sense as a first step. How can you address this in a productive manner that benefits you both?

Negative Person: I see your point. I must first find out why I am so terrified of being alone before determining how to do so. I must defend myself as well. My plan is to tell my husband, "I love you, but I can't put up with this. Please let me know when you're ready to treat me with respect." If he keeps treating me badly, I will leave his company.

How do the two of you now feel? How does it feel to perform at your best while inspiring others to do the same? This is the essence of positive thinking! Through practice, positive thinking will become as natural to you as breathing.

Positive Thinking and Success

Success entails a wealth of lovely, beneficial things. Success entails personal prosperity: having a nice house, going on vacation, experiencing new things, being financially secure, and providing your children with the most opportunities possible.

Success means liberation from worries, fears, frustrations, and failure. Success means having self-respect, greater levels of genuine happiness and fulfillment, and being able to do more for those who rely on you. Success means victory.

People in your work and social life will look up to you and admire you if you are successful.

Success, or getting things done, is the point of life. Everyone wants to be successful. Everyone wants the best that this world has to offer. No one wants to live mediocrely.

But if you want to be successful, you need to think positively. Having a "I'm-positive-I-can" attitude gives you the strength, skills, and energy you need to do it. When you think, "I can do it," you'll eventually figure out how.

Every day, young people in every part of the world start new jobs. Every one of them "wishes" that they will one day experience the success that comes with being at the top.

However, most of these people never get to the top. Because they assume it is impossible to reach enormous heights, they don't look for the means of doing so.

However, only a tiny percentage of these young people have genuine faith that they will be successful. When it comes to their profession, they have an "I'm-going-to-the-top" mentality. And because of their strong conviction, they succeed.

These people research and scrutinize the conduct of senior executives because they are convinced they will succeed and that it is not impossible. They gain insight into how successful people handle issues and make choices.

They study the demeanor of those who have already achieved success. The answer to "how to do it" is always there for the person who thinks he can do it.

Two years ago, a young lady I know made the decision to launch a sales agency for the sale of mobile homes. Many people told her she shouldn't and couldn't go through with it. They said that the minimum capital commitment necessary was far more than the five thousand dollars she had saved up.

She was warned that the environment was very competitive. Her advisers also questioned her lack of relevant expertise in the field, asking, "Have you ever even sold a mobile home, let alone run a whole business?"

But this young woman trusted in her own abilities and never gave up. She quickly admitted that she was short on funds, that competition in her field was fierce, and that she lacked relevant work experience.

"But," she said, "everything I've seen points to the growth of the mobile home sector. In addition, I've researched my rivals. When it comes to selling trailers, I am certain that I am the best option in town. Although I anticipate making some mistakes, I am confident in my ability to quickly get to the top."

Indeed, she did. She didn't have much trouble obtaining funding. Two investors put their faith in her because of her unwavering conviction that she could make the firm a success. And with a positive mindset, she accomplished the "impossible": she convinced a trailer manufacturer to advance her a small stock with no initial payment.

She sold trailers worth more than $1 million last year.

"Next year," she continues, "I anticipate making over $2 million."

Having a positive mindset motivates you to devise plans of action. And if you think you can achieve it, others will too.

This type of transformation is accessible to everyone. In this sense, positive thinking is always effective. Positive thinking can turn us from weak, negative, and indecisive individuals into strong, positive individuals. It can turn people from cowards to heroes, from soft-minded to tough-minded, and from criminals to heroes.

However, even though everyone has the power to change their lives with positive thinking, some people have trouble making it work. This is because they have mental blocks that prevent them from doing so. One of the mental blocks that comes up often is that they just don't want it to work. Some people simply don't want to do well in their lives. In fact, they are afraid of being successful.

It's easier to feel sorry for yourself. Thus, we bring about our own failure. and when a suggestion (such as positive thinking) is made to help us overcome that failure, we subtly try to ensure that it fails. Then we blame the concept rather than ourselves. But once we are aware of these negative mental responses, positive thinking starts to function.

Setting Realistic Expectations: The Journey of Positive Thinking

Most of us have high standards for ourselves. We must be the ideal boss, devoted partner, helpful friend, and forgiving parent. In addition, we should be able to maintain a balanced diet, get regular exercise, limit our time with electronic gadgets, enjoy life to the fullest, and find time to unwind and recharge. It just isn't possible.

While establishing high standards for yourself might be beneficial, it's crucial to make sure that these standards are realistic and attainable. Setting unattainable goals may, after all, result in disappointment, stress, and mental health conditions like depression and anxiety.

There are ways to return your expectations to reality through a combination of rational, emotional, and psychological techniques. Anyone can use these methods to have a better and more fruitful life.

In our 15-step journey to igniting our inner drive for excellence, we will learn how to cultivate a positive mindset. The first step is to rationalize our expectations. Here are some guidelines to follow:

Figure out what you value. Before putting all of your attention on all the things that need to be done, it's important to figure out what matters to you the most.

Each day is only 24 hours long. While that's not a lot of time if you expect to get everything done, it's plenty for work, errands, duties, and a few fun things.

Think about what you really care about. If you were to give each encounter in your day-to-day life a ranking, which would be at the top of the list? Do you make it a priority to be there for your kid's music lessons? Does picking up a cup of coffee at the corner cafe set you up for a productive day? Do you think about preparing for your natural sciences exam more than anything else? You alone know the answers to these puzzles.

There are only so many hours in a day, so establishing goals for what you want and need to accomplish most will help you prioritize your tasks. Think about what really matters to you.

Be open-minded. Expect the unexpected, and be ready to change your plans if something doesn't go as you thought it would. When things go wrong, take a deep breath and try to find an answer from a different perspective.

This is particularly true in the world we live in now, where things change all the time. Life is full of bumps and bruises, and just because you encounter some doesn't make you a loser.

Keep in mind that there is a distinction between your personal expectations and realistic expectations. Be flexible, and don't be so set in your ways that life's ups and downs create mental suffering.

Know where you stand. Not understanding your own limitations is a major roadblock to setting achievable goals. Know that you are not immune to defeat. Everybody has limitations, even you.

While defining personal objectives, take into consideration your mental and physical health. Don't put unnecessary pressure on yourself by expecting too much too soon. You will never be a comic book hero, despite your best efforts.

When we demand a lot of ourselves, we have to either be pleased with our achievements or disheartened by our failures. It's true that no one is perfect. And delegating is sometimes the only option to ensure that a task is completed to your satisfaction.

Is there anyone else you could collaborate with or seek help from? A close friend or family member who may not share your blind spot?

Instead of trying to do everything by themselves, a good leader would find out where they might use some help.

Avoid comparing yourself to others. It's quite natural to ponder why you haven't attained the same level of success as someone else after observing their achievements. They say there's always greener grass on the other side.

However, if you're prone to continual comparison, you may find that your anxiety, depression, and lack of confidence worsen very rapidly.

When you compare yourself to others, you are essentially attempting to conform to their ideals. You cannot force a square bolt into a round cavity, so maybe it's time to examine why you fail to see your own greatness.

This is where the problem with social media comes into play. The success and pleasure shown on social media are virtually always exaggerated. People only discuss the positive aspects of their lives, which sometimes makes us feel unimportant and left behind.

What we don't see are the problems and struggles they had to overcome to get there, as well as the one hundred shots they took prior to capturing the current, ideal image we see now.

Remember that you are on your own path and that what worked for someone else may not work for you.

Do your best, adapt as necessary, and have some courage. The objective is progress, not perfection. Go out and don't let your life become a formula; instead, live it joyfully. In the next chapter, we're going to learn how to develop a growth mindset.

Chapter 2 - Cultivating the Soil for Growth: The Power of a Growth Mindset

The Seed of Success: Understanding a Growth Mindset

What is the number one indicator of whether your business will succeed?

Is it the market, your ability to attract high-profile investors or the amount of money you invest?

None of these are right. In truth, if you lack one important element, a growth mindset, expanding your firm will be a painful slog, even when conditions are favorable. If you go behind the scenes of any successful business, you will discover an outstanding boss who has embraced a growth mindset. That's why I think the best way to tell if a business and its leader will be successful is to look at whether or not the leader has a growth mindset.

Having a growth mindset means you think and feel that you can improve your skills, knowledge, and emotional and social intelligence over time. Simply put, it indicates that you consider persistently overcoming obstacles to be essential to your success.

Leaders with a growth mindset are more concerned with the steps that lead to the desired result.

On the other end of the spectrum, we have a fixed mindset. This way of thinking says that core human features like skill and intellect are unchangeable traits. Fixated leaders are extremely goal-oriented and put a premium on getting things done. Instead of seeing a difficulty as an opportunity to learn and advance, they often view difficulties as failures, thinking that all their work has been in vain.

The following case study will help us dig deeper into these concepts.

Case study: Scaling up StarKids in England

PlayWonders and StarKids International have grown from 10 facilities in New Zealand to over 260 internationally in under 20 years, thanks in large part to Sophie Reynolds, Managing Director of StarKids International.

What was her secret? She possessed a growth mindset, which she instilled in her team. See how she helped David Parker, one of her team members, in his efforts to grow StarKids throughout England.

David worked as a banker on Wall Street for almost 20 years before becoming the master franchisor of StarKids in England. He had never worked with children before. Additionally, he was in his fifties, a time when most people would be preparing for retirement rather than launching a new venture.

A person with a fixed mindset would likely think that David lacks the necessary skills to be successful in the childcare franchise industry. He should be retiring after all; skills and expertise lie in the financial sector.

Thankfully, Sophie had faith in David's drive and potential for growth. She helped David refine his abilities and get access to StarKids in England.

Even David didn't believe he could learn new things. But because of Sophie's confidence in him, he signed up for the class she suggested. "I'm going to try it." David thought, "Perhaps an old dog can learn new tricks."

David cared only about getting better at things. "It helped me see things more clearly," he said. "It's not enough to know that I want to get from point A to point B. Now I know how we're going to get there, what road we'll take, and, most importantly, what car we'll be taking and who will be in it with me. I also have more time for my work and personal life."

What effect did David's growth have on StarKids?

Well, David eventually scaled StarKids in England. From Manchester to Birmingham and London to Liverpool, people who were interested in buying StarKids franchises got in touch with him. David set out to make StarKids available in all 48 counties of England within 5 years, now that he knew there was a real need for this product or service.

Only Sophie's growth mindset, which encouraged and supported her team to enhance their abilities and the company, made this accomplishment possible. The story of Sophie and David demonstrates how employers with a growth mindset inspire their employees to do the same.

Planting the growth mindset: Changing your perspective

To transform your perspective into a growth mindset, you need to develop a sense of purpose. Do you think your life has a point? If yes, write down exactly what you want to achieve. If you can't think of anything, spend some quiet time thinking about your "purpose" and see what insights arise until you feel like you have a handle on it. Then work toward it; that's the path to developing a growth mindset.

Flip criticism on its head until you find the good in it. The goal of criticism is to improve things. Someone else can look at what you are doing from a different angle than you can, and they may have suggestions that are useful to you. You can cultivate a growth mindset by being receptive to their feedback.

To change your perspective into a growth mindset, you must welcome challenges, keep going even when things don't go as planned, own up to your mistakes, and know that hard work is the only way to get good at something. This is the main idea behind the adage, "Practice makes perfect."

There are two main reasons why it's important to have a growth mindset. First, it helps those in charge come up with a fluid plan, honing their ideas continually and seeing opportunities where others see threats. The second reason is probably less apparent but no less important: a business that adopts this sort of mentality and makes it a part of its culture will become more productive. Because the management gets more out of its workers. In fact, the belief that people can build latent skills and become more valuable for the company can significantly alter how the company works from the inside.

Managers with a fixed mindset treat people under them in accordance with how they perceive themselves: as superior islands in a sea of mediocrity. Now, several studies have shown how unworkable and constrained this strategy is. These businesses make hires based on an applicant's personal qualities and the state of their existing skill set. In such a "culture of talent," people are selected based on their strengths and weaknesses, which limits their potential and hampers the company's development.

Managers in such an environment tend to favor a small group of employees and ignore the rest. Because of this dynamic, low-performing workers may give up, bend over backward, or even cheat to advance in their careers. Also, managers with a fixed mindset can easily resort to domineering and aggressive behavior when they feel threatened by the success of their employees. The lack of feedback prevents employees from growing. As a result, disappointment and mistrust grow, eating away at the business from the inside.

Managers who adopt a growth mindset, on the other hand, help their team flourish and receive more in return, which benefits the entire organization.

These leaders train their employees, recognize and reward progress, provide constructive criticism, and see setbacks as teaching moments.

Here are some real-life examples of a growth mindset:

Madam C.J. Walker: C.J. Walker, whose given name was Sarah Breedlove, was born in 1867, an era when it was very rare for a woman, much less the daughter of freed slaves, to become a prosperous entrepreneur. There were moments when C.J. Walker might have had a fixed mindset and just tried to make the most out of the situations she found herself in. She lost her parents when she was 7 years old, lost her husband when she was young and started losing her hair because of a disorder affecting her scalp. Walker demonstrated her growth mindset in this final challenge. She might have accepted her condition for what it was, but instead, she invented a treatment that could reverse the effects of the ailment, launched her own line of hair care products, and amassed a fortune as a result. She ultimately decided to contribute a significant portion of her wealth to charitable causes within her local community.

Jack Ma: Jack Ma was the only applicant out of twenty-three who was turned down for a job at KFC, and he failed his college examinations three times.

That's when he started Alibaba, a business that struggled for many years but is now quite successful after 25 years of tremendous effort.

Here are some examples of Fixed-mindset:

Lee Iacocca. Lee Iacocca was furious that he was forced to leave the Ford Company when Henry Ford II was appointed to lead the organization. Then, in an effort to win Henry Ford over, he fixed up Chrysler. Even though he was successful, he was always worried about how people saw him and afraid that his less important workers might get more praise than him. Consequently, the Chrysler Corporation suffered.

Nokia: This well-known mobile manufacturer stubbornly refused to switch its phones to the Android platform, allowing Samsung and other rivals to quickly catch up and overtake it. As a result, Nokia experienced a decline and fell behind in the mobile market.

Cultivating Your Growth Mindset Garden: Practical Steps

To continue sparking our inner drive for greatness, the second step is to learn how to establish a growth mindset.

To meet the challenges of the ever-evolving digital world, today's most successful leaders have a common trait: a growth mindset. The following practices and ideas may help you develop a growth mindset for both yourself and your team.

Accept Change

Modern leaders who are most successful accept that we live in a rapidly evolving digital environment. They prepare themselves to drive meaningful change by welcoming it rather than avoiding it. This may include changing their own behavior, that of their team, the organizational procedures, and structures, or even the overall mission and vision of their company.

Know yourself

Before we can make changes and grow, we need to know where we are now. What are our personal boundaries, what drives us, and what are our emotional states? When you know more about yourself as a boss, you are better able to make important choices and look for ways to grow the business. It will also help you figure out where you and your team need to improve.

Disrupt Yourself

You are prepared to interrupt yourself after you have achieved self-awareness. The author of The Potential Principle, Mark Sanborn, argues that leaders should disrupt themselves before an outside force does it for them. If change comes from somewhere else, like new technology, you may find it hard to keep up and adjust. But if you are the one who drives creativity, you are the one who changes the game.

To cultivate the habit of disrupting yourself, be ready for change, and adopt a growth mindset, Mark suggests asking yourself the following questions:

What patterns of behavior, rituals, and routines in your life need to be altered a little?

Are you relying on strategies that used to be effective but aren't producing the same results (if any) today?

Are you wasting time on meaningless pursuits?

What other uses of your time would be more beneficial?

How much of your day do you spend fantasizing as opposed to doing what has to be done?

Is there anything you can do to stop worrying about less important things?

Are you wasting time on meaningless relationships? Do you need to adjust your interactions with a bad influencer, set boundaries, or cut ties altogether?

By making a deliberate effort to disrupt yourself, you initiate the process of transformation in your life. This transformation will manifest in your ability to foster a team with a growth mindset.

Acknowledge the importance of learning from mistakes

When it comes to managing a company, failure is always a possibility. Leaders who reflect on their shortcomings and incorporate those lessons into their toolbox are more likely to push themselves and their teams to new heights. It's also crucial to foster an environment where mistakes are seen as opportunities for growth. This will inspire your team to learn and try new things.

Keep in mind that the process is a work in progress

One of the basic tenets of the growth mindset is an emphasis on effort rather than outcome. No human being or business will ever perform flawlessly all the time. There will be times when the outcomes fall short of expectations. This is why it's crucial to pay attention to the procedure as well. By concentrating on the process, you will strengthen your team and make small but steady gains in performance.

Be persistent

It takes time for an oak tree to reach a height of 40 feet. Success happens when you put in your best effort and patiently wait for it. So, if you learn to embrace setbacks as challenges and keep going when things get tough, you'll enjoy greater influence as a team leader.

Finally, don't allow your ego to prevent you from making positive changes in your life. When you adopt a growth mindset, you'll challenge yourself to go beyond your current level of competence and confidence. The ego hates it. But if you listen to it, you'll end up just like everyone else.

Therefore, if you want to stand out and achieve your full potential, be willing to overcome your ego, fixed mindsets, and self-imposed boundaries. In the next chapter, we'll learn about the perils of a negative mindset and how to overcome them.

Chapter 3 - Breaking Down Negativity's Walls

Understanding the Power of Negative Thoughts

Negative thinking is our enemy. It saps our spirits, dries out our excitement, and makes us less productive. It makes us confused, slows us down, makes us put things off, and can even cause us to lose sight of our goals. It thwarts us. It baffles us. It is responsible for the "bad luck" that we would later lament.

When we give in to our negative thoughts and tell ourselves things like, "It's not going to work out," "I have bad luck," "There will be a problem," "So-and-so will happen, and it will only make me feel worse, so why bother?", we are our biggest enemies of success.

Every day, our minds produce anything from 25,000 to 50,000 thoughts. If the mind is stuck in a never-ending loop of negative thinking, imagine how many thoughts it generates every day- thousands upon thousands! Negative thoughts have a snowball effect, causing more negative thoughts to follow in their wake. And "Now" is as good a time as any to break free from this cycle and not let these negative messages control us anymore.

A big problem here is that negative thoughts slip into the brain under the radar of conscious awareness and turn into powerful habitual patterns. They appear automatically and quickly before we do anything about them.

On an unconscious level, however, having negative thoughts is a way to protect ourselves so that if something bad happens, we won't be caught off guard and crushed by it. By preparing for loss, we think we can make it less painful if it does happen.

Sadly, this is not a sound strategy. The negative anticipation of misfortune and failure contributes to their occurrence by preventing us from putting forth our best effort. It hampers the flow of positive energy and causes the Law of Attraction to attract negative outcomes as opposed to positive ones.

It deepens our worry and anxiety and reduces our belief in ourselves and our abilities to achieve our goals.

In this way, thinking negatively is a kind of self-abuse. Of course, anticipating potential challenges and developing a plan to overcome them is crucial to success. However, self-punishment occurs when we allow our fearful, negative thoughts to paralyze us, preventing us from taking on challenges and failing to achieve our goals so that we can avoid feeling disappointment, embarrassment, or humiliation.

Remember, allowing ourselves to be derailed by worry and anxiety will never result in a life full of unicorns and rainbows. In this chapter, we're going to discuss the types of negative thoughts our mind experiences and how to overcome them.

Identifying Our Thinking Errors

In this section, we're going to learn how to spot negative thoughts and manage them. The first step in managing negative thoughts is to know that they exist. Thinking errors are negative thought patterns that lead to erroneous perceptions of the world. Everyone has them, but if they are reinforced often enough, they may raise anxiety, deepen depression, and lead to a variety of other disorders.

These distorted thoughts occur as a way to deal with bad things that happen in life. The longer and worse the bad things are, the more probable it is that one or more thoughts will arise. When you engage in negative thinking, you'll frequently experience some of the following thinking errors...

All or nothing

When we adopt an "all or nothing" mentality, we get fixated on attaining perfection at any cost. Our brains tell us, "Either I do it perfectly, or I don't do it at all." We strive for excellence by forcing ourselves to work harder. We tend to be quite hard on ourselves because of the high standards we set for ourselves, which may lead to worry or anxiety. We seldom attempt new things because we are afraid of failing miserably. We begin to feel that nothing is ever good enough, which causes us to be frustrated.

Overgeneralization

When our brains are clouded by overgeneralization, we see each negative occurrence as a never-ending cycle of setbacks and failure. Based on one isolated instance, we may generalize about all situations. For example, if you fail an interview and don't get the job, you can extrapolate that failure and conclude, "I will keep failing interviews and never obtain a job."

As a result, the next time you are invited to an interview, you may unconsciously assume a poor outcome based on your past unfavorable interview experience. Overgeneralization causes undue stress.

Selective abstraction

Another flawed habit of thinking that holds us back is "selective abstraction," or mental filtering. When this mental filter is turned on, individuals focus on the bad elements of any circumstance while ignoring the good. They seldom perceive the brighter side of life, as if they are wearing negative glasses that screen out the positive parts. They tend to assume the worst, even in trivial situations.

Diminishing the positive

When you have this negative thought pattern, you turn positives into negatives by negating the positives. You tend to dismiss a great experience by claiming it does not count for one reason or another. In your mind, you could be rationalizing that it was just a lucky occurrence. People who are quick to downplay the good are inconsistent in their approach, hence unable to provide a rational explanation of a topic. They give weight to counterarguments, even if they appear illogical or irrelevant, and disregard positive evidence regardless of how compelling and convincing it seems.

Jumping to conclusions

The tendency to jump to conclusions is very prevalent among negative thinkers. They often jump to conclusions about people or situations without having any evidence to back them up. A negative thinker just thinks this is true without looking into it first. This thought pattern can be put into two groups: mind-reading and telling the future.

The capacity to read another person's thoughts is not innate. Still, we can't help but try to guess what someone is thinking. Negative thinkers often think that other people think they are dumb or boring or that they are being looked down on.

Have you ever caught yourself frequently having thoughts like, "My supervisor must be mad at me," "My subordinates must be thinking I'm insane", or "My colleagues must think I'm lazy?" If so, instead of using definite language, frame your assertion as a hypothesis (they might think).

One further example of "jumping to conclusions" thinking is the practice of fortune telling. When a negative thinker looks into the future, all they see is suffering. "There is nothing to look forward to; there is no use in holding out hope, and despite my best efforts, I will inevitably fail."

Or your subconscious may also make dire forecasts like "I won't get hired for that position" or "It's going to be a bad day today." Negative thinkers turn these kinds of thoughts into strong beliefs by saying them over and over in their heads.

The binocular trick

With binoculars, things far away look closer and bigger. But if we look through the wrong end of binoculars, everything looks far away and smaller. When we're in a negative mood, our thoughts play tricks on us. It's as if we're wearing special glasses that make us see bad things as more significant than they really are and good things as more minor than they really are. Because we are used to the binocular trick, we unconsciously give more weight to perceived failure, weakness, or threat and less weight to perceived success, strength, or opportunity.

Catastrophization is a type of magnification in which a negative thought is blown out of proportion and makes the negative person feel very upset. For example, you may have made a small mistake at work and worry that it will cause you to lose your job. When we focus too much on the negative outcomes that may occur in the future, we are more likely to assume that "it's bound to all go wrong for me."

Emotional reasoning

When we are in a negative mood, we may let our emotions decide what to do. The idea behind emotional reasoning is that what you feel must be true. We can get past most thinking errors by thinking logically, but it's hard to do so when we're thinking emotionally. If we keep ignoring the dark thoughts that make us feel bad and try to make decisions based on our emotions, we may get lost in the maze of depression.

In emotional reasoning, we use feelings instead of facts. The underlying premise for this thinking error is that "if there is smoke, there must be fire." For instance, "I feel bad. I must have done something wrong."

If we make choices based on emotions, it can be quite harmful to our mental health. Feelings or emotions are not proof of reality, just as smoke is not conclusive evidence of fire. We must learn to analyze our feelings and determine if they are real.

Should and must statements

Statements like "should" and "must" are frequent negative thought patterns that negative thinkers experience. People with a negative outlook on life often use words like "should" or "must" in their sentences. These words emerge as the mental result of guilt. When a negative person makes a should or must comment towards themselves or others, they often feel angry, guilty, resentful, or frustrated.

Using these phrases often can be very damaging to a person's mental health. These statements often emerge unconsciously and instinctively. Here are some examples: "I should never get upset with my partner" and "I feel bad about the speech I just delivered. So, I must be a terrible public speaker."

These claims often result in irrational expectations, which may raise anxiety.

Labeling and mislabeling

Negative thinkers are prone to applying derogatory labels to both themselves and others around them. Mislabeling and labeling are extreme examples of generalization. We all make mistakes, but we either forget them or figure out what went wrong and move on. But people with a negative mindset construct a sense of self out of unpleasant experiences. As a result, they may begin to believe they are losers. Negative thinkers may also judge others unfavorably. In this case, they could unintentionally foster negative feelings like animosity, envy, and hate. Most of the insulting labels that the negative mind uses are not true. These labels come from a skewed view of how things really are. This thinking error hurts self-esteem.

Personalization

People with this thinking error take things personally. They may feel personally accountable for other people's rage over failure, bad weather, or a number of other things they can't control.

When their parents get divorced, teenagers with this thinking error may feel guilty because they think it's their fault. A severe personalizing tendency may lead people to believe they are responsible for almost everything. When a problem arises, they immediately think, "I must have done something wrong." They may also examine the situation obsessively to find a reason to blame themselves.

Break the Cycle of Negative Thoughts

Now that we know about thinking errors, we can spot them as soon as they arise and deal with them effectively. When people are overwhelmed by negative emotions like worry and guilt, these negative thoughts come up on their own. But instead of trying to avoid them, we have to learn to deal with them sensibly. It takes a certain amount of mental energy. We all have that strength, no matter how weak we think we are. Remember, when we try to get away from our own thoughts, we unintentionally give them more power and let them make our lives hard.

Negative mind encourages either/or (black and white) mindsets that lead us to categorize ourselves and other people as "good" or "bad," "right" or "wrong," "winner" or "loser," "intelligent" or "stupid," and so on. When we adopt such dualistic perspective, we begin to live in an absurd world of extremes

If you have mood swings because of these black-and-white thoughts, figure out how to deal with them in a logical way. Here is how to do it:

Suppose you are having an extreme thought: "I am an idiot."

Replace this thought with something less rigid, like, "I can be smart and still do something dumb."

Ask yourself, "Do I really believe I'm stupid or a loser?" Attempt to clarify these phrases, then ask yourself, "Do these terms really describe who I am?" Have a logical conversation with yourself every day.

Review the should and must statements when the mind starts persuading you that you have to do or be something. One possible response to this mode of thinking is provided below.

Evelyn gets nervous when she thinks about flying. Her employment, however, requires flight travel once every three months. Every time she has to go to the airport, she has an intensely unpleasant conversation with herself. It goes something like this: "There's no reason for me to feel this anxious. I'm an adult, for goodness' sake! I don't understand why I can't relax while flying. I have to get past my fear".

Evelyn is clearly being unreasonable with her expectations of herself. By being so hard on herself, she's only setting herself up for future disappointment.

There is a more effective way for Evelyn to deal with her fear than using should or must: "It's true that I'm nervous right now, but I'm doing my best. I know that getting better takes time, so I'm not in a hurry. Every day, things get better. I'm working on getting over my fear, and I'm okay with where I am in the process right now."

When we get trapped in the vicious cycle of mental errors, we spiral downward and feel like our lives are falling apart. But when we break free from the negative cycle, we unlock our victory code and reclaim our personal power. In the next step, we're going to learn how to overcome negativity through visualization.

Chapter Two

Chapter 4 - Picturing Prosperity: The Power of Visualization

Unveiling the Power of the Mind's Eye

Where do you want to see yourself in five years? What do you see your future partner looking like? How much money are you expecting to make? If someone questioned you in this manner, what kind of response would you give? To put it another way, have you resolved everything up to this point? Great! If that's the case, you may skip this section.

But if you're still uncertain about how to answer all the questions, you're not alone. The good news is that there is a powerful tool that can help you do so: it's called visualization, or the mind's eye.

The Cambridge Dictionary defines visualization as the process of imagining something or someone in your mind. It's as if you were gazing at your life from the inside out, but through the lens of your subconscious, your imagination, and your innermost aspirations.

Visualization is more of a deliberate activity that has a plan and a goal. The key to effective visualization is to engage all five senses in order to bring your mental picture to life and completely immerse yourself in the associated emotions.

Most techniques you may use to influence and rewire your subconscious mind rely heavily on visualization because the subconscious mind understands and responds to images more than anything else.

Some studies revealed that thoughts generate the same mental commands as actions; mental images have an influence over most of our cognitive functions, including attention, perception, planning, and memory. That is to say, the brain does not distinguish between an activity in one's mind and an actual action.

When you do anything, you're stimulating a certain set of neuronal circuits and triggering the release of a certain set of neurotransmitters. When you imagine yourself doing something, it triggers the same physiological and chemical responses as actually doing it.

Sportspeople have been using visualization techniques for decades. Muhammad Ali was a true believer in the power of visualization. He was so sure about the potency of imagination that he confessed, "If my mind can conceive it and my heart can believe it, then I can achieve it". He wasn't the first athlete, however, to employ visualization to his advantage. Arnold Schwarzenegger shared this belief and often visualized himself looking exactly as he desired. He then applied this method to his pursuits in politics and acting. Research published in Neuropsychologia showed that picturing moving certain parts of your body is almost as good as actually moving them. The human mind indeed holds immense power.

Visualization and financial success:

Various visualization techniques can be used to increase your chances of monetary success. Many successful people used visualization techniques to break their limiting beliefs and attitudes toward money.

When you have negative thoughts and beliefs, like "I'm terrible with money" or "There's no way I could ever afford it," you'll find it difficult to make good monetary choices. Visualization will help you change these distorted mindsets. You'll start believing in your ability to save, invest, and spend wisely.

Another visualization technique is imagining your goals and working towards them. When you visualize yourself setting and achieving your goals, you can start to believe in your ability to achieve them. This can not only make you more motivated and determined to get it done, but also help you understand the steps to reach your goal, as well as how to deal with any problems that might arise. We will talk about it in more detail in Chapter 7.

You can also use visualization to develop positive habits. Habits like setting aside a certain amount of money each month, making a budget, and contributing to a retirement plan can help your finances grow and stay stable over time. Visualizing your habits will make you confident in your ability to maintain them, which is important for financial success.

Mastering the Art of Visualization

So, how can you put this into practice? How can you harness the power of visualization and get all of its benefits?

The idea of visualization is simple: imagine the scene in as much detail as possible, using all of your senses (sight, sound, smell, touch, and taste). Some people find it easier to focus if they close their eyes, while others find it easier to write everything down instead of doing it all in their minds. As there may not be a "mental imagery switch" (yet) in any of our heads, there are several methods for easily entering the "visualization mood".

Meditation is one of them, and if you're looking for guided meditation, the one below is a good place to start.

Let's prepare for the meditation session. Get yourself into a comfortable posture and settle your body into its natural state. You can sit or lie down. If you're in a sitting position, place your palms on your laps, one on top of another, with palms facing upward. If you're lying, place your hands by your sides, palms facing the ceiling.

Close your eyes. Allow your awareness to merge with your body and breath. If thoughts arise, note them and let go.

Now, with your mind's eye, visualize yourself on a beautiful sunny day outside in a nature sanctuary. This could be a tranquil tropical island beach, a flourishing old garden, or maybe a beautiful secluded green forest where the bright rays of sunlight are gleaming through the trees. Take time to visualize in vivid detail.

As you're taking the imaginary nature walk, feel the firmness of the earth beneath your feet or the soft grass. Observe the various colors of the leaves and the shapes of the tree limbs.

Hear the birds singing in the trees, and smell the sweet fragrance of beautiful wildflowers. This is the place where the healing center is located.

Enjoy the beauty as you walk along the narrow, shadowy forest trail that leads to the healing center.

The healing center is a hexagonal white marble building. It has large domed windows.

Before you step into the healing center, spend a moment standing at the door and observing what's inside the building.

As you walk in, feel the soft carpet beneath your feet. In your healing center, you have all the healing tools, from ancient to modern, at your disposal to cure any kind of ailment.

Spend a while looking at those tools, touching them, and figuring out how they work.

At the other end of the room, there is a healing chamber. You can think of the chamber as a small phone booth.

Inside the healing chamber, there is an instrument panel with buttons and levers to activate the treatment.

Enter the healing chamber and sit comfortably in the sitting machine.

Press the bright yellow sunshine button, which zaps a million volts of healing current into your mind and body.

Feel the healing currents.

Imagine that when the shockwaves of healing energy hit negative emotions like fear, anger, resentment, and guilt, they cause tiny explosions and turn into positive energy.

Imagine the healing current destroying the power of harmful memories to bring about negative thoughts and emotions.

all your sorrows are melting away. All your inner conflicts are disappearing.

The healing process is now complete. Now we'll let go of the mantra and become aware of the sensations in your body.

Gently step outside the healing chamber and walk up to the exit. Now it is time to leave this magical world.

Take a slow walk along the road that leads towards the real world.

you've reached the end of the road, and an interdimensional doorway has appeared.

Step into the doorway. Feel the process of transitioning into the real world.

Now imagine a gentle breeze is blowing

Breathe in deeply. And exhale

One more time:

Open your eyes. Expand your awareness of your surroundings. Stretch your hands and legs.

Overcoming Visualization Roadblocks

It is very natural to feel certain discomforts while practicing, both physically and mentally. Distractions and annoyances are necessary components of meditation. We call them "weeds." They will appear and disappear at different degrees and intervals.

Here are some typical distractions that may arise throughout your meditation:

Restlessness: It's normal to feel unsettled when you meditate. Restlessness can be a sign of buried memories and unsolved issues in the unconscious mind. It can also be a sign of the unconscious mind trying to cover up some deeper level of experience.

Drowsiness: Feeling sleepy or fatigued during mediation is a common problem. In the beginning, the mind does not like the process of meditation; so it generates the urge to sleep to avoid practicing. There are a few things you can do to help the mind stay awake during your practice:

Get adequate night-time sleep

Avoid practicing after a heavy meal.

Open your eyes slowly and take on a mindful gaze. Gently look around without being distracted by the surroundings.

Holding your breath is a quick fix for drowsiness problems. Take a deep breath and hold it as long as you can, then release slowly. Repeat this process until the drowsiness fades.

Let go of the urge to try hard: Until the process of visualization becomes spontaneous, you'll need to apply a little effort. But make sure to maintain relaxed and steady efforts. Don't force yourself to imagine anything or put in exaggerated efforts— there is no place for violent striving. The moment you find yourself struggling, be aware of your struggle and let go.

Remember, being good at visualization takes time. Visualization is not something you master overnight. Take as much time as you need; there's no rush. Hurrying will delay your progress. Relax and pretend you have all the time in the world.

Have self-compassion. Don't fall into the trap of perfectionism. We all have our flaws, but you should remember that you are all you have. Be gentle with yourself. The moment you totally accept yourself the way you are, the process of transformation begins.

In the next chapter, we're going to learn about the Law of Attraction and how to leverage it for success.

Chapter Three

Chapter 5 - Creating Your Reality. The Law of Attraction and Positive Thinking

Understanding the Law of Attraction

The purpose of our existence is to live a life of harmony, love, and abundance. We all crave love and fulfillment, and we are designed to thrive, not just survive. It's our true nature to get everything that life has to offer. But we focus so much on the negatives in life that, unconsciously, we choose a life of unhappiness, discontent, and frustration.

We work hard because hard work brings fortune. But no matter how hard we try, fortune remains out of reach. So, we keep hoping that something miraculous will happen that will magically change everything, but that never happens.

Why do our deepest wishes never come true? Why don't our dreams remain unfulfilled? The Law of Attraction has answers to these questions.

The forces of attraction are present everywhere. They are present in every object, from the smallest atom to the largest star. If you look at an atom, for example, the basic unit of all matter, you'll find that they attract one another by a pull of attraction known as the intermolecular force to form molecules. Analyze the atom using an electron microscope. You'll see that within it, an invisible force of attraction is making electrons rotate around the nucleus (proton and neutron), much as our earth revolves around the sun or our solar system circles around the center of the Milky Way galaxy.

Much like the ones between massive celestial bodies and tiny atoms, the human mind also has an attractive force. In fact, our minds work like magnets, drawing into themselves the situations and orchestrating the events that determine our fate.

Our mind creates our world through perception. It's our perception that draws people, objects, and events into our lives. That's why people with similar interests become friends, confident people become financially successful, and people who think negatively bring conflict and misery into their lives.

Our perceptions of things and events often become the only factor determining how they will impact our lives. For example, if the thought of being in an interview makes you nervous, you may tell yourself things like, "I'm terrible at interviews," or "This one definitely won't go well." Unwittingly, you're creating a negative vibration within yourself, which will reflect in your body language, your tone of voice, and also in your verbal messages. As a result, you might not do well in the interview. Because your self-defeating inner conversations brought your fear into existence. This is only a small case, though. Everything that happens in our lives is a mirror of our perception of the world.

The first rule of the law of attraction is, "Like thoughts bring about like events," or "Like attracts like". So, whatever you are thinking about, you are unknowingly drawing it to yourself.

Most of our thoughts lack the force necessary to become realities. But unconsciously, we empower our negative beliefs through negative self-talk. Unwittingly, we develop such firm faith in them that we bring them into reality. In fact, most of our misfortunes can be traced back to our misuse of the law of attraction.

But the good news is that if a negative thought has the potential to become a physical reality, a positive thought also has the same power. Positive thoughts are, in fact, more potent than negative ones. We can flip the mental compass if we turn our attention away from failure toward success.

Everything that happens outside of us is an expression of our inner world. What happens within our minds controls our physical world. Therefore, if you want to be the master of your own fate, you have to master your inner world.

Things that don't exist in the mind also don't exist in the real world. So, in order for anything to happen in your life, you have to cultivate that desire within you.

The Relationship Between the Law of Attraction and Positive Thinking

Thinking positively is a choice, and of course it plays a huge role in using the Law of Attraction to attract the things we desire. But that's only a piece of the puzzle.

Let me explain. If you choose to spend the whole day making sure that your thoughts are positive but your beliefs are mediocre, you will not be able to attract what you desire.

It's because while your positive thoughts will certainly act as magnets, drawing in the things you want, your mediocre beliefs will act as a wall, barring your path.

If your entire day is spent thinking positive thoughts and in the evening you decide to meet a friend to complain about life, you are not a match for what you desire.

Become aware of your thoughts and feelings and find out if the way you feel matches what you think or believe; if not, you will need to work on not only what you think but also what you believe and how you feel.

I don't want to downplay the importance of thinking positively. Because without it, it's not possible to build the life you want. Learn to think positively, and soon you'll start to feel positive and believe positively.

Keep this in mind every day as you go about your life. Your thoughts will become things only

when your thoughts, feelings, beliefs, words, and actions are in harmony.

Just a bad thought popping into your head is not going to make something bad happen right away.

As soon as you spot a thought that does not support you in creating the life you desire, replace it with one that feels better.

Leveraging the Law of Attraction for Success

Now, you have a clear understanding of the law of attraction. Let's learn how to use this powerful law to attract your heart's desire and transform your life. Follow the steps below.

1. **Know what you want.** The first step to materializing your desire is to know what you want. Are you absolutely sure about what you want? Is it clear in your mind? If not, take time to reflect on it. When you've made up your mind, ask yourself why it is that you want it.

For example, if what you want is a house on the beach. Ask yourself, "Why do I want it?" Do you want it just to impress people? Or do you want it because the sound of splashing waves gives you a sense of peace, and you enjoy the smell of the sand? Ask yourself, "Will it really make me happy?" Knowing the qualities of your wants will make you consider ways to obtain things beyond material possessions.

Now, make it a realistic objective in your mind. Ask yourself how big your house should be, how many bedrooms you want in your house, and if you want a garage with it.

Take some time to answer these questions. Don't rush.

Define what your desired life should look like. Remember, to manifest things, you'll need to have a clear vision of what your future life would look like if you had that object.

1. **Remind yourself.** The next step is to reinforce your vision of the future. Take a small step every day to remind yourself that you are heading towards your vision. If you have no idea where to start, take a trash bag and start decluttering your house. Pick up all the unwanted items lying around and put it in the bag. This may sound strange, but getting rid of material clutter is a good way to signal the subconscious mind that you are letting go of the attachments of things that

are burdensome, and no longer serve you. It not just signals the change, but gives you a fresh start, an opportunity to reinvent your life.

If it doesn't sound appealing, grab a pen and paper and write about your desired future life. Be precise, do not make a general statement, and be as elaborate as you can. The idea is to remind yourself of your vision. Because every time you remind yourself what you want in life, the energy or the vibration of your vision will get stronger.

1. **Practice gratitude:** To use the law of attraction in a positive way, you have to nurture positive qualities and noble virtues. You can't attract anything positive with negative energies like greed or arrogance. So, feel grateful for what you have. When you are grateful for what you have, you attract more of what you have and what you desire to have. But if you spend most of your time thinking about what you don't have and complain about that, you are inviting negative forces that will attract more reasons for you to complain about. That's why, in this stage, we will express our gratitude to the universe.

Maintain a journal or notebook, list two or three things you feel good about, and express your gratitude for having them in your life. In time, the feeling of gratitude will be stronger, and it will attract more things to be grateful for.

1. **Visualize:** In chapter four, you have learned that the subconscious mind can't distinguish between reality and a vivid imagination. That's why if you put a clear image before your subconscious mind, it will believe in it. And that image will appear in real life. Visual imagery meditation is the most effective way to do that. For practicing visual imagery, make sure you are in a quiet place and won't be disturbed for the

next twenty minutes. Sit down comfortably in a chair with your hands on your lap and your feet apart from each other.

Close your eyes, take 3-4 deep breaths, and exhale slowly. Relax your body from head to toe. Feel that your body is getting loose with every inhalation.

Now imagine that you have been shifted into your future life. Imagine vividly, but don't try hard. Visualize the life you ever wanted to live. Imagine from the first person's perspective and be one with your imagined self.

Add color and texture to your imagination. Hear the sound. Feel the touch..., and participate in activities you want to take part in your future life. For example, if your goal is to become the head of a company, imagine how you're going to spend your time in your workplace. Imagine yourself holding an important meeting with your managers.

You may also imagine your future social life ... the wonderful moments with your partner...or the vacation in exotic destinations.

In the beginning, you may not see a clear image. No worries! Bring the feeling, and the image will follow. There is no struggle here. You don't have to be perfect at this. In time, the image will be clear.

Take all the time you need, and when you're done, take a couple of deep breaths. Then, softly open your eyes.

Don't share your vision with anyone. You don't have to believe anything yet. Just stick to your practice and reinforce the image in your mind. The universe will do the rest.

Addressing Common Misconceptions about the Law of Attraction

Misconceptions about the law of attraction may prevent people from using it efficiently and getting the benefits. Here are some common misconceptions about this spiritual law.

The Law of Attraction is the law of greed

Some people want to believe that Law of Attraction programs are get-rich-quick scams because they promote the notion that you can attract and have whatever you desire. But there is a lot more to the Law of Attraction than meets the eye, only if you invest the time to learn about it.

Greed is a negative emotion, whereas the cornerstones of the Law of Attraction are positive feelings like gratitude, love, abundance, positive thinking, awareness, self-discovery, and being in the flow. Greed typically drives people to want more and more, whereas the Law of Attraction teaches that you should begin by being content with what you have and feeling grateful for it.

The law of Attraction demands lots of effort

Learning to gain mastery over your thoughts and life's events will certainly take effort. Yet, this shouldn't place you in a position of hardship. In fact, it can even help you live a better life.

When you're a traditional thinker, you just passively accept whatever comes your way. Where proponents of the Law of Attraction teach you to center your thought, direct your path, and create your own reality.

Not everyone can use the Law of Attraction

You may discount the Law of Attraction in an effort to avoid confusion. But the Law of Attraction affects every single being on earth, whether you choose to be aware of it or not. So the idea that the Law isn't for everyone is absurd; it's like saying gravity doesn't work for everyone or that fire doesn't always produce heat.

Fire will always be hot to the touch, gravity will always pull us toward the earth, and the Law of Attraction will always bring us that which we give our attention to. The more we learn about it and find out how to use it to our benefit, the better off we'll be.

But don't panic, thinking you're attracting something you don't want simply because you've thought about it for a moment.

In the next chapter, we're going to learn about the power of positive affirmation and how to incorporate them into our lives.

Chapter Four

Chapter 6 - The Power of Positive Affirmations

Understanding the Power of Affirmations

An affirmation is literally anything you say or think. But most of the time, what we say and think is not very positive and doesn't make us feel good. That's why we need to change our thinking and speaking into positive patterns so that we can bring positive changes into our lives.

An affirmation opens the door for change. When you practice affirmations, you are consciously choosing words that will either help eliminate a problem from your life or add something positive to it.

Every word you say to yourself in your inner-talk is an affirmation. You're constantly using affirmations in your mind, whether you're aware of it or not. And with every word and thought, you're creating your reality.

Each of your complaints about life is an affirmation. Every time you get angry, you confirm that you want more anger in your life. Each time you feel miserable, you're affirming that you want more misery in your life. If you feel like a victim and think that Life isn't giving you what you want, you confirm that you don't want to get what you want from life.

There's nothing wrong with the way you think or feel. And having these negative thoughts or feelings doesn't make you a bad person. You've just never learned how to think positively about yourself.

From the theory of the law of attraction, we've learned that our thoughts create our experiences. But most of our parents probably didn't know this. So, they taught us how to look at life the way their parents had taught them.

However, it's time for us to wake up and start making positive changes to our lives by restructuring our thoughts.

We can do it. We just need to learn how.

Practicing Positive Affirmations

Practicing positive affirmations every day will boost your self-confidence and motivate you to move forward fearlessly.

Set aside a few minutes of your day to practice the following exercise. Make sure you're not in a hurry.

You'll need a full-length mirror so that you can view your entire image (if you don't have one, a bathroom mirror or handheld mirror will work fine). Stand in front of the mirror naturally, just as you normally do. Try to look confident. To do that, align your shoulders with your legs. Now your feet are directly under you, just a few inches apart.

Make sure your weight is distributed evenly on both legs. Straighten your spine and hold your head up.

Now take a deep breath and push your chest forward. Exhale and push shoulders back— not way too far back. Keep your arms relaxed. The aim is to look relaxed yet aware and confident. When you are ready, take a couple of deep breaths and look at yourself in the mirror.

Now say the following affirmations to yourself:

I'm getting ready to welcome the success.

I'm the powerhouse.

I'm connected with the universal mind.

I deserve to enjoy prosperity and affluence in my life.

I have limitless potential.

I'm a success magnet; I attract success in whatever I choose to do.

I'm receiving infinite abundance.

I'm the creator of my reality.

I'm worthy of love, abundance, happiness, and success.

I'm feeling the positive change.

Nothing is impossible for me.

I'm the person that I was meant to become.

I envision my future and take action to make it happen.

I have all it takes to make positive changes in my life

I believe in myself

I choose to be happy and successful

Every day, I'm getting closer to achieving my goal

Look confident while saying these affirmations out loud. Remind yourself to say them with conviction. Speak in a slow, relaxed manner so that the mind can totally grasp the message. Don't rush. Don't practice when you're in a bad mood. Speak to the mirror as if you were speaking to a good friend. Be loving, kind, and nurturing.

Crafting Your Own Positive Affirmations

Although there are no hard and fast rules for creating affirmations, there are still a few guidelines to make them better. Here they are:

Try to write in the present continuous tense whenever possible.

Although we normally write affirmations in the present tense (unless we're writing specifically for the future), the present continuous tense makes them more effective. Look at these two statements below:

I chose to pursue my goal.

I am choosing to pursue my goal.

Although both of them sound positive, the second one sounds more real and in the present. It gives the impression that you're already in the process of achieving your goal.

However, you can't just force any affirmation to be in this tense. What matters most is that it should generate a feeling of motivation and positive emotion in you.

Make sure they are focused on your goal.

What do you want to work on? Have you already set your goals? Do you have a career goal, a health goal, or a relationship goal? Create separate sets of affirmations for each goal.

An affirmation for obtaining a desired job can look like, "Every day, I'm getting closer to my dream job."

Here is another example of an affirmation for the goal of improving your body image: "I'm loving and accepting my body just the way it is."

So, write down your goals and make 2-3 affirmations for each of them.

Make them concise

To make the affirmations work, you'll have to repeat them over and over to yourself. So, create affirmations that you can easily remember and say at any time. They should sound precise and focused on your goals. Keep it simple and avoid mixing many things together.

For example, if your goal is to sleep better, write, "I am going to have a sound, peaceful sleep tonight."

Add emotive words to make them powerful, such as excited, joyous, happy, eagerly, smoothly, and strongly.

Adjust yourself.

Where are you in your life now? Can you describe your current state of mind? How easy is it for you to switch to a positive state of mind and agree with the affirmations you repeat?

We're all at different stages of our journey. So, create affirmations that sound convincing and suit your purpose. Affirmations must be directed towards your goal, but make sure your mind doesn't find them hard to accept. For example, someone who's confident in his abilities and enjoying a successful life can easily say, "I know that I am the best version of myself!"

But someone who has experienced some failures may need more empathetic affirmations like, "I'm slowly and confidently heading toward my goal."

Incorporating Affirmations Into Your Daily Life

There are many ways to develop a positive mindset, and you've already practiced some of them in the previous chapters. But positive affirmations are one of the most simple and accessible ways to set yourself up for success.

To easily incorporate positive affirmations into your daily life, it is important to pick affirmations that really resonate with you. The affirmations should not only be directed at your goals; they should also provide a direct response to your frequent negative self-talk.

Many people don't create their own positive affirmations. Instead, they adopt affirmations they see others using. This is also a good way to start, but to get the most out of positive affirmations, you need to create ones that are centered around the goals you've set for yourself.

For example, you're frequently experiencing self-talk like, "I'm good for nothing" or "I can't do this." and you want to regain your confidence. In this case, you would create a positive affirmation that would eliminate those negative affirmations, perhaps something like "I believe in my ability" or "I have what it takes."

When you approach positive affirmations in this way, they will appear in your mind whenever you experience negative self-talk and defuse it. That means the moment you say to yourself, "I can't do this," your subconscious mind will immediately respond with, "I have what it takes."

Go beyond the repetition. Although affirmations work for most people, sometimes you may find that simply repeating your affirmations isn't giving you enough motivation, and you need to learn more about them. If that is the case, feel free to supplement your affirmations with other learning tools. Read books on the topic of your affirmations (body positivity, healthy relationships, productivity, etc.). There are lots of resources on the internet. Watch documentaries, and TED talks, listen to Podcasts, read blogs and articles, and use them to your advantage.

You can also maintain a notebook to write down the insights you've had, the things you've learned, and your comments on your progress. They will be particularly helpful
when you start to notice the progress in your mindset and your actions.

Staying Motivated and Committed

Using affirmations to set a life goal and working toward it is certainly a big step toward improving your life. But staying motivated and achieving what we've set out to accomplish is not easy, especially when negative emotions like boredom and frustration are draining your energy, and you just don't feel like working.

No one can always stay motivated; we all lose motivation from time to time. When you feel negative emotions are tiring you out and decreasing your motivation, use the following suggestions to get back on track.

Ask yourself why

Sometimes, your why—the reason why you're doing what you're doing—matters more than the what or the how. Becoming clear about why you want this can be enough to stimulate you to stay on course.

Create a clear vision

We've already discussed it in Chapter 4. Putting a clear vision in front of your subconscious mind will keep you focused on your goal. So use visual imagery meditation to create a clear, compelling vision that you can relate to and resonate with. Keep in mind that it will only work if it speaks to your heart.

Choose success

Success is a choice, so choose to be successful. Maintain a success mindset until you reach your goal. Imagine success using the visual imagery technique you've learned. It will increase your chances of being successful.

Try to have fun.

Fun is a great motivator that will keep negative emotions at bay and make you feel energized. So, chase after your dreams and have fun while doing it.

Finally, don't forget to reward yourself, even for a small accomplishment. Setting up a system of rewards for the completion of small goals will motivate you to stay on target.

In the next step, we're going to learn how to build wealth through positive thinking.

Chapter Five

Chapter 7 - Charting Your Financial Freedom Path

S etting Your Financial Goals

People define financial freedom in different ways. It is not very easy to have your own definition of financial freedom because it forces you to ask many questions to find out what really matters in your life. For me, it is a state of mind where I'm free to make choices about life without worrying about the financial implications- where I have the ability to do things I love. Where I have the freedom of not having a boss, and my life doesn't depend on some opaque company's whims. Financial freedom does not necessarily mean retirement, but it does mean doing things on my own terms.

To attain financial freedom, it is important that you set your money goal, then align your intentions with your actions and direct your actions toward that goal.

So, let's start with setting your own money goal. Follow the steps below:

1. The first step of goal-setting is to write it down. Because the moment you write your goal on paper, it becomes concrete. As your goal is to obtain money, write down the amount. You can write any amount you want, but keep in mind that you must feel deserving of obtaining it.

2. Now, write down the things you'll spend the money on. If you have no idea, you may try the following brainstorming exercise:

In your notebook, write down what you want to brainstorm in the form of a question (in this case, "how I'm going to spend my money?"). Take a couple of deep breaths and write down whatever answers come to your mind. Write all the answers down. You may find some of the answers silly, even impossible. But don't skip them: write them down, too. Keep your pen moving, and don't judge your answers. After you're done, you will discover that you have something to say.

1. By now, you have a list of things you're going to spend your money on. Your next step is to rank them in terms of preferences. You can now eliminate some of the items from your list if they don't sound very realistic. These are your goals. The item you've ranked highest is your top goal.

2. Now check if your goals meet the following criteria:

The goals are specific (they are well-defined, clear, and unambiguous). You can visualize your goals because you're very clear on the specifics, which explains the features of your goal.

The goals are measurable, so as you move forward with your goal, you can review your progress at any time and know when the goal is reached.

Your goals are realistic. They sound achievable. For example, the goal of becoming super-rich in a month is not a realistic goal.

When your goal setting is complete, you are ready to continuously work on your goal until you reach there.

Building a Positive Mindset to Attain Wealth

The journey towards getting rich starts with changing the way you think and believe about bringing an abundance of wealth into your life. It starts from within. Most of us are not aware that wealth is a state of mind, and as soon as we shift into that state, opportunities will appear out of thin air.

Of course, obtaining abundant wealth is not an easy journey. It takes smart planning, hard work, dedication, and patience. And when you have a smart plan, and you're ready to work hard toward your goal, you'll get support from the environment and luck. Not random good luck. You may call it "opportunity luck," which occurs when you stretch your thoughts and expand your abilities.

Financially successful people frequently experience opportunity luck. You'll also attract opportunity luck into your life when you believe in yourself, become determined, and explore ways to reach your ambitious goals. Opportunities will appear before you when you are obsessed with your goals and do what is necessary. Some of the opportunities will occur quite unexpectedly.

In this section, we'll learn how to develop a positive wealth mindset to build wealth and attract opportunity luck. To do that, you need to change some of the beliefs that are deeply ingrained in your psyche. And the first step in doing that is breaking unhealthy patterns of relationships with money that weaken your ability to prosper. Spend some time understanding your money behaviors, spending triggers, and your financial self-image. Think about how you interact with money, manage, and talk about money. Also, explore why you always take a certain approach to spending, saving, and investing.

Remember, no matter how your relationship with money is, you have the ability to change it, although it needs some inner work because it took ages to develop.

First, learn about your current unconscious wealth programming by completing the following sentences:

1. I'd have more money if_____

2. Money causes_____

3. My biggest financial fear is_____

4. I'm scared that having more money will_____

5. My parents always believed money would_____

6. Money is_____

7. Money makes people_____

8. Rich people are_____

9. If I were a wealthy person, I would_____

10. The biggest challenge for becoming rich is_____

11. If I want to have more money, I have to_____

Now, take a look at your answers; they will be the indicators of your current mindset about money. From your answers, identify any of your unconscious money beliefs that might be obstructing your financial progress, even if they don't seem unquestionably "true" for you. If you do this exercise every day for a week, you'll gain more insight into your unconscious wealth programming.

Analyze your answers, and find out if your unconscious beliefs and associations with money are those of someone who is programmed to be poor or rich.

Remember, your thoughts and beliefs about money, the words you speak while in a conversation about money, your money decisions, and most importantly, what you feel about money in the privacy of your own heart and mind dictate the nature of your relationship with money.

Now, think about the emotional relationship you have with money. Does money flow into your life naturally, or is there any sense of having to work hard or of struggle? What are the dominant emotions that arise in your mind when you hear the word money? Do they lean in the direction of favorable feelings like ease, comfort, and abundance or in the direction of distressing feelings like insecurity, anxiety, and frustration? Deep down in your heart, do you feel a sense of abundance and a feeling that your needs are always being taken care of, or do you feel a sense of inadequacy no matter how much you have?

You need to find out these answers to understand your money mindset.

To change your views and beliefs about money, you don't need to change anything in the outer world. Your inner world will change when you develop awareness through self-inquiry.

By elevating your awareness of your mindset about money, you can start to make sense of many of your money behaviors and emotions and take steps to reframe them. It is important that you liberate yourself from the deep-rooted beliefs that prevent you from taking appropriate financial risks.

Heal yourself from your financial regrets. Forgive yourself for all the bad financial decisions you made in the past. We all made bad money decisions in the past. Many of them bring a sinking feeling of guilt and regret every time we think about them. Unfortunately, sometimes we allow our past mistakes to define us. We become extremely self-critical when it comes to money. While in isolation, we regret what we did or didn't do.

I've made so many money mistakes in the past— things I wish I did not do. But I had to move past the hurt and pain to build a better life for myself.

To be able to forgive yourself, you'll need kindness, empathy, compassion, and acceptance. Whenever you find yourself obsessing over regrets, examine the emotions attached to the memory of the mistakes— let go of the emotions. If you struggle with letting go of the emotions, acknowledge out loud— "This is fear," "this is guilt," "this is anger." Don't try to change your emotions. Just acknowledge them and let go.

Don't deny your mistakes or blame them on others— own them and fix them if possible. Accept the fact that, inevitably, you'll make mistakes again. Know that every time you make a mistake, you will have the courage to forgive yourself and learn from your mistake.

Face your money fears head-on. Spend at least one hour every week thinking about the money you have. Review your checking and savings accounts and credit card balances. Embrace your current financial situation.

Money has such a powerful impact on people's lives that it is tough to get away from the influence of it. The sudden gain or loss of money can greatly affect people's behaviors, attitudes, and personalities, even their physical well-being. When you have a healthy relationship with money, you won't feel overwhelmed by your money problems. It is really hard to improve your finances when you feel miserable. A healthy relationship with money will help you to feel more in control and bring forth solutions that may not have been apparent with the stress.

Now whisper any ten of the following affirmations to yourself in the morning before you start your day:

Everything I touch turns into gold.

Money flows spontaneously and abundantly.

My actions create constant prosperity.

My mind is in harmony with the energies that generate money.

My good comes from everywhere and everyone.

I'm focused on achieving wealth.

I can easily generate money-making ideas.

I'm divinely guided and protected.

I'm positive about money and happy with the money I have

The amount of money I can possess is limitless

With every passing moment, I'm getting richer.

Every day, I'm getting comfortable with the idea of having a lot of money.

Every day and every way, I'm getting richer and richer.

I'm at peace with money.

I'm a powerful money generator.

I rejoice in others' luxury and success, knowing there is plenty for us all.

My relationship with money is improving every day; I'll keep making as much money as I need.

The money I spend comes back to me in multiples.

I am fully open and receptive to the abundant flow of riches that the universe offers.

All is well in my world.

Harness the Power of Vision

Having a clear vision is paramount to creating your desired wealth. All the greatest entrepreneurs in the world had clear visions. A vision will motivate you to explore, take challenges, and break through barriers. It will inspire you to persist, to persevere, and to succeed. Everything is created twice— first in your vision, then in your reality.

Believe in your vision. If the negative voice in your head discourages you and tells you that you don't deserve your dream, don't challenge it. Be compassionate and kind to yourself, and gently remind yourself that the voice is not really out to sabotage you; it actually tries to protect you. But you're strong now. You've learned to crush your comfort zone and grow toward the very life you dream of.

Be grateful for the finances you have right now. It will cultivate the right money mindset and attract opportunity luck.

To win the game of getting rich, first, you have to win the inner game. The inner game is about eliminating self-doubt and instilling the belief that you have what it takes to become rich.

Chapter Six

Chapter 8 - Charting Your Career Course with Positivity

The Power of Positivity in the Workplace

Let's face it: Work has to be done. In the workplace, what separates people from one another is how they approach their work- it doesn't matter whether you are an employee or an entrepreneur. Approaching work with a positive mindset can be one of the keys to accomplishing your task effectively and improving your overall work experience.

When you develop a positive mindset, it will benefit everyone, including yourself, your employees, colleagues, and customers. By having a positive outlook at the workplace, you help create a supportive environment that fosters productivity and personal growth.

Having a positive mindset at work has many other great benefits. It transforms the way you view your work and the way your coworkers and customers see you. Below are some of the advantages that a positive mindset at work can offer:

It decreases your stress level: When you have a positive outlook, you perceive challenges as minor setbacks that are manageable. It makes you feel much happier and more capable of managing professional obstacles. A positive outlook also doesn't let you dwell on problems when they arise. As a result, you can maintain a good mood and keep your stress levels low. This helps you thrive in your career, even when it is demanding.

It improves your productivity: People's brains function at their best when they think positively. If you start thinking positively, soon you'll find an increase in your energy levels, which will make you feel more alert and energized to perform your duties. You'll also be able to think clearly and focus on the task at hand because of the reduced stress level.

You become good at problem-solving: When you are a positive thinker, you can look at multiple possibilities for solving a given problem. This problem-solving ability is useful for everyone, from managers who want to get the most out of their employees to engineers developing new products.

It encourages skill development: Positive thinking makes you an open-minded person who can easily learn from coworkers and develop new skills by joining formal training programs. As an open-minded person, you'll also be more willing to try something new because positive thinking makes you a quick learner.

It boosts your decision-making ability: As positive thinking puts you in a good mood, stress can no longer impact your judgment. As a result, you can make clearer and better decisions. In time, your confidence in making the right decisions improves. You begin to believe that no matter how big the problem is, things will resolve satisfactorily in the end.

You become better capable of seizing opportunities: The positive outlook will enable you to take advantage of opportunities in your workplace, like promotions and training programs. Because when you're a positive thinker, you are more confident about breaking your comfort zone than your negative-thinker counterparts. You'll no longer view opportunities as threats but rather as chances for advancement. You'll know for sure that you have the knowledge and ability to handle these workplace challenges. The ability to spot opportunities when they arise gives you a greater chance of career success than staying in the same job and never taking a risk.

It makes communication easier: People naturally gravitate to positive-minded individuals, and this makes building good relationships in the workplace easier. Having good relationships makes positive thinkers more easily communicate with their colleagues and subordinates than others might. When you can efficiently interact with others, teamwork and networking become much easier. You'll find more people who agree with your ideas and professional goals.

It helps in conflict resolution: When positive thinkers receive feedback, they use them to improve themselves. When they face conflict, they turn them into opportunities for growth and improvement. They use feedback to discover their strengths and weaknesses to become better employees. They accept the fact that people have different views, and not everyone will agree with them all the time. This helps them keep conflict in perspective. They can patiently listen and learn from people with whom they disagree.

It makes you more resilient: You can't expect everything to always go your way even when you have a positive mindset. Accepting this fact will help you put the challenges in your career in perspective and motivate you to move forward with a determination to succeed.

Applying Positive Thinking at Work

Work can be challenging and stressful. Because you not only have to meet deadlines and goals but also show great work. Sometimes it takes a toll on your mental health. In times like these, negative thoughts and emotions can creep in and affect the quality of your work. But maintaining a positive attitude during these times can make all the difference.

Here are some powerful methods for having a positive attitude at work:

Give recognition to your team

Connect with your team members in a meaningful way. You may email a co-worker and thank them for their help or support. This recognition can work like a charm and motivate them to work harder. You may also acknowledge some of your teammates in a public forum while rewarding them for a job well done. This will create a positive and inspiring work environment.

Avoid complaining

You can easily maintain a positive attitude when things are going your way. But a challenging situation arises, and things don't go the way you want them. During these times, it can be hard to stay positive and avoid complaining. But complaining won't make the problems go away. Instead, maintain your calm and take time to think through the situation. Enquire if there are any underlying issues behind this problem and how this problem is affecting your workplace.

Remember, sometimes, what seems like a problem is not an obstacle at all. Therefore, take time to clarify if you have identified a real problem. Things may appear problematic when we approach them with a negative mindset, which does not allow us to see the whole picture.

You may also recognize something as a problem, which is only a surface problem with many underlying issues. In this case, if you just tackle the surface problem, ignoring the underlying issues, you are only applying Band-Aid to your wound. This may help heal your wound for the time being, but the wound will reappear many times in the future until you fix the underlying causes. That's why we have to work on the cause rather than the troubles that the cause has brought forward.

Therefore, inquire about the origins of your problem. Ask yourself who is to blame for this problem and who perpetuates this trouble. You can write down the answers.

Win people over

Have you ever gone the extra mile for someone important to you? Have you noticed how their face brightens up when you do so? If you want to win one's heart, make them feel special. Appreciating others can change their views towards you. But if you make someone feel that he or she is irreplaceable, you will instantly win his or her heart. Take time to listen to people you care about most, value their input, compliment them, and make them think that they are an important part of your life. You will be rewarded with the same response. Whatever feeling you transmit, it comes back to you, sometimes in manifolds. By making others feel important, you can create a strong bond with people.

If you are an employer, make your employees feel that they are a valuable part of your organization. Let them know that they are fascinating and they have a lot to offer. In return, they will work with utmost sincerity to meet the organization's goal. If you are a salesman, make your clients feel that they are really important. A positive attitude with warmth in the voice is absolutely priceless. If you overlook the customer experience, the business will suffer. Enchant your clients and let them fall in love with your business; you will be amazed by the result.

Positive Communication at Workplace

With the help of positive communication, you will be able to connect to everything that will contribute to your growth. People will naturally like you and establish you as someone who is trustworthy and a great person to work with if you are gracious with your words, as you are outstanding in your performance. Positive communication eases the gaps that arise between individuals who have very little or almost nothing in common.

In order to master the art of positive communication, it is important to know your strengths and weaknesses in areas like conversation style, attitude, physical presence, personal revelation, and response to others. Ask yourself the following questions:

Conversation style: Do you enjoy a long conversation or prefer limited talk time?

Attitude: Do you try to appear as a positive individual, or do you bring whatever you are feeling to the social occasion with you? Are you confident about your social abilities?

Physical presence: How do you generally feel about your appearance? Do you think a change in hairstyle or wardrobe boost will put you in the right mood for socializing?

Personal revelation: How comfortable do you feel talking about yourself? Some people can easily reveal personal information; others are very careful about revealing themselves. Do you comfortably talk about your skills and expertise?

Response: What is the nature of your response to others? Do you think that you are perceived as friendly, kind-hearted, and supportive?

Reviewing these essential personality areas can improve your ability to intuit how people see you, and this helps you to authentically connect with other humans and obtain the deep satisfaction that comes with those ties. Often, we negatively judge our personality type and think of it as unchangeable.

Here are some guidelines for effective positive communication:

Overcome your conversation-killer attitude. One of the common attitudes that ruin the conversation is the thought that a conversation has to be an argument. Managers with this attitude first determine how their point of view differs from that of their counterparts, then pick it apart in favor of their own "superior" point of view. They always tend to "prove" their counterpart is wrong, no matter how rational they sound. If the arguer is not especially tactful, he may say, "Well, I think that's a stupid idea," or "Who told you such a thing?" or "Do you really believe that?" They are almost always on the defensive side, and their mantra is "I object." Next time you are talking to a co-worker or employee, observe your response when they say something with which you disagree.

Pay complete attention when you are conversing with someone. If you are inattentive or overthink what you want to say next, your response may not make full sense. If your phone is ringing during the conversation, don't be too quick to answer the phone. Take a while and say politely, 'I'm sorry, but I have to take this." Some people find it annoying when we talk on the phone in the middle of a discussion. An ideal conversation should be back and forth and engaging. Paying total attention means being completely present.

Being a patient listener is crucial for effective communication. Not everyone is a good listener. And not everyone listens with the true intention of understanding the message. People often listen only to reply. Therefore, take the time to listen. Listening can help you to identify more common grounds and generate more topics of discussion. Some people look for listeners because it makes them feel better when they have someone to listen to their stories of success and glory. They seek admiration and acknowledgment when they deliver talks of their achievements. Listen to their stories and admire them; they will quickly turn into your good friends.

Smile. People easily get more attuned to positive emotions than negative emotions. A smile conveys positive energy. The easiest way to attract people is to greet them with a nice smile. We smile when we meet people, introduce ourselves, and when we say goodbye. Some studies showed that most people are very good at distinguishing a sincere smile from a fake one. A real smile is contagious and quickly spreads in the faces of the audience. Most people can't ignore a real smile. So, smile from your heart. However, the frequency of smiles will be different when we are socializing than when we are interacting with our subordinates and bosses. Therefore, smile when it is appropriate.

In the next chapter, we're going to learn how to foster positivity in relationships.

Chapter Seven

Chapter 9 - Planting Positivity Seeds in Your Relationships

The Ripple Effect of Positive Communication in Relationships

'What can make a relationship work'? The answer is quite simple. Couples, who are really happy in their relationship, are not smarter than average human beings. They truly care about their relationship and are willing to put time and effort into it. They intrinsically perceive their relationship as a process rather than something to be simply "fixed" when it goes wrong. It makes them less afraid of their difficulties.

Any seasoned financial adviser would encourage you to invest your money regularly to secure your financial future. A relationship also requires regular investments from both partners to make it thrive. Also, similar to a business, a relationship has ups and downs. There might be times when having a great partnership seems effortless (like when your business is generating profit without even trying). And there will be instances when, despite your efforts, things feel like they are heading bad ((like when the values of equities go down). If you want to succeed, you have to persist in times of difficulty and find your way through obstacles.

Every relationship that works has one thing in common— positive communication. And every single relationship that doesn't work, has communication issues. A good relationship thrives on thoughtful communication, which requires being available to talk, listening actively to the other person, and expressing your needs as kindly as you can.

Try to pick a time when you're both available to have a calm discussion free from any distractions. When it's not the right time to talk, let him know. Express yourself kindly, sensibly and with ease. When you express yourself kindly, you create a warm and intimate atmosphere. This will make it easier for your partner to remain calm and hear what you have to say.

Remember, most marital arguments can't be resolved. Couples sometimes find themselves in endless and useless rounds of arguments. They spend year after year trying to change each other— but it can't be done.

Invest time and energy in your relationship to make it thrive. The time and effort you put into your relationship are one of the best returns on investment you can have. Support each other's hopes and aspirations and build a sense of purpose in your life together.

A key component of happy individuals is "psychological flexibility." So be flexible. When you're flexible, you can easily absorb the disappointment and continue to care for each other. This can enhance your relationship.

The attitude of total commitment is also a very important element of a successful relationship. It's easy to feel committed to your partner when things go well. But when things get tough, it is common to feel overwhelmed by the amount of anger and frustration. In those moments of desperation, some people even think that it might be best to just walk away from the relationship. So instead of focusing on the problem, focus on the solution to show your spouse that you are committed to your relationship.

Fostering Positivity in Relationships

What image comes to your mind when you think about an ideal life together as a couple? Do you have an image of a romantic young couple strolling side by side at dusk on an exotic, tropical beach?

Do you picture a life filled with happy moments, laughter, fun and adventure?

You may have an image in your head about what a good married life should be like. This image might have been formed unconsciously based on the Hollywood movies you've watched, or romance novels you've read... and when you look at your relationship, it does not match your vision of an ideal married life.

So. if the fantasy image we have in our mind is not a perfect relationship, then what is it? We'll find the answer throughout this chapter. But you can start constructing the real image right now by letting go of the notions of your dream relationship.

Your fantasies will keep you trapped in the labyrinth, thinking about how you'll escape one day and find the perfect married life ever. You'll have too high of hopes for your partner, which will keep you from fully appreciating them. You'll begin to see all the flaws in your spouse and may complain about his imperfections.

Here are some of those common statements people make when they have unrealistic expectations of their partners:

"I wish my husband/ wife were more attractive."

"I wish he were more honest and transparent with me."

"I wish she were wildly attracted to me and had eyes only for me".

"I wish he could spend more time with me."

"I wish she agreed with everything I said."

If you want to nurture a fulfilling life together, you must get beyond those unrealistic expectations. One of the great ways to do that is to focus on the positive qualities. Grab a pen and paper and write down five greatest qualities of your partner.

Now answer the following questions:

1. When you met your partner for the first time, what were the qualities that made you attracted to her more than any other?

2. What is the happiest moment you've had with your partner? Describe it in a few sentences.

3. What are you thankful for in your partner? List five things you might be thankful for.

4. What are the good things people say about your spouse?

Imagine the wonderful images of your happy moments with your partner. Stay with these images for a while. If the negative thoughts arise and your mind wanders, re-read your answers.

Overcoming The Relationship Barriers With Positive Mindset

You may seek endless qualities in a soul mate like no piece is missing from the puzzle, but do you know that the qualities that truly matter are few in number? If you envision your perfect partner to be an utterly magnificent male/female, a paragon of perfection and set unrealistic expectations about love, you may not find one. Ask yourself a simple question to test the health of your current relationship: "Am I frequently lonely?"

In a relationship, it's not unusual to feel alone. You can feel lonely with your partner when you're experiencing emotional disconnection with him, the chemistry is gone and your relationship is no longer flowing. You can overcome these issues with a positive mindset. But before that answer the following questions to find out if your relationship is moving at a healthy pace.

1. Do you feel like you're more lonely now than you were before you got together?

2. 2. Do you feel unheard and unloved?

3. Do you feel like your partner judges you?

4. Can you and your partner truly put aside your differences and forgive one another?

5. Does your partner like hearing your thoughts when you have anything to say??

6. Is she supportive of things that you do?

7. Is he aware that you have a life of your own?

8. Does he tell you what to wear and how you should look?

9. Do you struggle to articulate your needs and feelings to her?

10. Does she make you feel like no one else would want you?

11. Do you feel uneasy with him or as if you're "walking on eggshells?"

12. Do you feel physically and emotionally safe with her?

If your answer is Yes, your score is "1"; if the answer is No, the score is "0". Now calculate your total score. If the score is above seven, then your relationship is not working as well as it should. In this case, you've to determine the root cause of loneliness.

Sometimes our unwillingness to be vulnerable often contributes to this feeling. Our own negative thoughts can often make us lonelier than a person or the situation. Sit alone with your thoughts and find out if your negative mindset is making you feel lonely. Sometimes a simple mindset-adjustment can fix the problem.

Sit down with your partner and talk. Tell him/her what you think or feel about the current state of your relationship and find out if he's feeling the same way. Listen to his response— be patient. Allow him as much time as he needs to talk. Don't argue, justify, defend or explain. Check to see whether you and your partner agree on the need to repair the relationship, then find out the factors that damaged your relationship and ways to make it better. You may also consider seeing a couple's therapist. Be positive. Remember, there are always ways to make the relationship work. And it is possible to turn a regular relationship into a soul mate level.

In the next chapter, we're going to learn about the healing power of positivity.

Chapter Eight

Chapter 10 - Invigorating Wellness. Positive Thinking for a Healthier You

The Healing Power of Positivity

The way we think has a major impact on our physical and mental health. People who frequently experience negative thoughts and feelings show higher levels of cortisol, a stress hormone that is produced in the body during challenging situations. Over time, this excessive release of stress hormones can lead to bad health outcomes, including higher blood pressure and heart disease.

But it isn't just the release of stress hormones that affects health—the very perception that stress affects health also does!

One study indicates that it isn't necessarily unusually high stress that increases the risk of mortality but rather a high level of stress coupled with unhealthy (negative) thoughts and beliefs that lead to negative health outcomes.

In fact, people who believe negatively about themselves and their health are more than twice as likely to die from heart failure compared to those without beliefs and thinking habits.

On the other hand, people who have a positive attitude toward life not only feel happier but they also enjoy better physical health in almost every way. They have fewer physical symptoms, such as common cold, fatigue, and sore throats, and recover from surgery more quickly and with less discomfort.

They have less chance of getting both major and minor illnesses, including ulcers, diabetes, hypertension, flu., asthma, and even coronary heart diseases and strokes.

Even more interesting, one study demonstrates that patients with a positive outlook on life undergoing chemotherapy for ovarian cancer experience a larger decline in cancer markers.

Many experts believe that positive people enjoy better health partly because they experience less stress. They use adaptive coping mechanisms in the face of challenges—tackling problems head-on, seeking social support, looking on the bright side, and so on. Their proactive approaches to stressful situations reduce their negative effects and the physical toll they take. As a result, people with positive thinking habits, like seeing the glass as half full, have stronger immune systems, which makes them better prepared to fight minor diseases.

In one study, researchers examined the levels of happiness in 193 healthy adults before and after voluntarily receiving a cold virus through nasal drip.16 (Remember, healthy individuals normally recover from cold.) Soon, the participants began to experience cold-related symptoms, such as coughing, sneezing, and runny nose, which lasted for four weeks.

But despite being directly exposed to the cold virus, many of the volunteers didn't become sick.

In fact, those who had a more positive view, in general, had fewer cold symptoms and were less likely to get the flu. These results remained true even when researchers took into consideration other factors, including age, sex, body mass, and general health, that may influence susceptibility to sickness.

Improving your Health with Positive Thinking

Positivity is just an honest way of looking at life. It helps you improve your emotional adaptability so you can see the good in others and let go of things you can't control. You already know some of the health benefits of positive thinking. In this section, we're going to learn how to improve our health with positive thinking.

We'll start with studying your habits. Sometimes, we unwittingly create thought patterns and habits that hinder our ability to think positively. So, I recommend you track your habits for just one week. Write down your daily activities and routine. Make sure to include:

When you eat breakfast, lunch, and dinner, as well as what you eat at each meal.

When do you become physically active, and for how long?

When do you get ready for bed, and what is your bedtime routine?

How many hours do you sleep, and how do you feel when you wake up?

When you wake up in the morning, what is the first thing you do?

How much time do you spend on screens during the day, and how do you feel afterward?

Feel free to update the information any time during the week, and at the end of the week, look for the habits that encourage or prevent you from thinking positively. Some of the habits, such as brushing our teeth, taking a shower, reading a book, or taking the dog for a walk, make us feel refreshed. If these patterns encourage positive thinking and feelings, you don't need to change them. Instead, give yourself some credit for making these good choices.

But if your habits are making you feel bad, it's time to change them. Now grab your notebook and form two columns. Under column one, list your bad daily habits. Under column two, list their opposite habits, which will be your new positive habits. Here is an example.

Bad daily habits	Good daily habits
I waste so much time on social media (Facebook, etc.)	I limit myself to 30 minutes of social media per day.
I watch TV while eating food	I get rid of all distractions and enjoy my meal.
I don't exercise regularly	I exercise 30 minutes every morning
I procrastinate	I make sure to accomplish every task on my to-do list every day.
I smoke	I won't smoke anymore.
I go to bed late every night	I'll go to bed between 9-10 pm
I don't return phone calls right away	I will return every phone call today
I always run late to appointments and meetings.	I will always arrive 15 minutes earlier before an appointment or meeting.

Breaking bad habits and adopting healthy ones is not easy. That's why you'll need to exercise your willpower and self-control to change your habits.

There is a common myth that it takes 21 days to form a new habit. The truth is that the amount of time needed to develop a new habit depends on several factors, including the person, his or her behavior, and the circumstances. It can take up to two months or more before a new behavior becomes automatic.

Follow your new habits for the next thirty days and review them once in the morning and once before you go to bed. Create a checklist. The target is to accomplish around 80% of your daily good habits.

Daily good habit checklist (sample items)

1. I woke up at 6 o'clock today.
2. I jogged for 30 minutes today.

3. I limited myself to 15 minutes on Facebook today.

4. I arrived at my office 10 minutes early today.

5. I did not waste time on the internet today.

6. I spent 50% less time on personal calls, e-mails, or tea breaks today.

7. I completed 80% of my to-do list today

8. I didn't put off doing my work today, even the project I dreaded.

9. I consumed no more than 2000 calories today

10. I kept my personal problems out of my workplace today.

11. I said, "I don't know," instead of giving a wrong answer when I was asked a question and I truly didn't know the answer.

12. I left the office at 5:30 pm today

13. Before leaving the office, I prepared my task list for tomorrow.

14. I limited myself to one beer today.

Replace your lost needs. If you're giving up something, you've got to do something else to adequately replace the need you lost. For instance, if watching TV gives you a way to relax, you could take up relaxing music or meditation as a way to replace that need.

Eat the right foods and work out

If you don't feel physically well, it's hard to stay positive.

Therefore, to maintain a positive mental state, take care of your physical health by consuming nutritional foods and doing regular exercises.

I don't recommend giving up all your favorite foods; just be mindful about what you eat.

But make sure to include fruits and veggies, lean protein, and complex carbohydrates in each meal. Also, try to stay as active as possible.

If this sounds too much, start small. Avoid eating between meals, but if you must, go for fiber-rich snacks like apples, cut vegetables, or low-sugar granola bars instead of unhealthy foods.

Do some exercise every day, but make sure you enjoy it—whether it's strength training, walking, yoga, or swimming. Regular exercise burns stress hormones like adrenaline and cortisol and helps you stay positive.

If you have pain or other physical conditions keeping you from exercising, work with a physical therapist to heal your injury and look for alternatives, such as chair exercises, to stay physically active.

You don't have to make drastic lifestyle changes in a week or two; make small choices to stay fit to help sustain a lifelong path of positivity.

Practice mindful eating

What we put into our bodies has an impact on every aspect of life, including positive thinking. But do you know that our decision-making about food is very complex and that there is a wide range of internal and external stimuli that influence our food choices?

It's not just your physiological drive toward food that tells you that you need to eat to keep your body fueled, but rather a complex set of physical, emotional, and cognitive stimuli that lead you to grab that tasty snack even if your belly is full.

Mindless eating stems from negative thoughts and emotions. The emotional hunger that causes the overconsumption of food can easily become chronic, have serious health consequences, and affect our thought processes.

Positive eaters consciously nourish their bodies with healthy foods. They know the art of mindful eating, which you're about to learn.

To practice mindful eating, it is better to choose a quiet environment. Always reserve a certain time for meals. Put away all the distractions and turn off the TV.

Sit gently and slow down your movement so that you can watch the entire process carefully without judgment. Allow your mind to settle down, and take a while to allow the body to recover from the day-to-day toils.

Bring your awareness to your breath, body, emotions, and thoughts— don't cling to or resist any thought, feeling, or emotion. Instead, notice the whole domain of your life and accept everything with a non-reactive awareness.

Smile softly and become aware of the smell coming from the food in front of you. If you are having meals with others, smile in your mind and take a good look at the food. Name the foods in your mind, like salad, peas, and so forth. It is important to feel grateful while eating because the foods are keeping you alive and nourishing your body.

You don't need to think about your food. However, in some mindful eating workshops, participants are asked to ponder the origin of the food as well as the process of growing, transporting, and preparing it before focusing on the physical aspects of the food.

Now begin to eat. As you take your first bite, be aware of the sensory experience of chewing and tasting. What does the food feel like inside your mouth? Is it moist or dry? Hard or soft?

Enjoy the food with all your senses— savor every small bit. You may close your eyes to explore the sense of touch, smell, and taste of the food inside your mouth. Analyze the different tastes and flavors you detect. Chew mindfully and thoroughly.

Feel all the textures of the food and become aware of different aspects of your experience, one sense at a time. Don't haste. Eat slowly— feel as the food travels along the food pipe. Don't over-eat and avoid overanalyzing. And once you are done, feel satisfied and content.

Cultivating Mental Resilience Through Positive Thinking

Sometimes, our uncomfortable inner experiences (a thought, emotion, or craving) force us to give up our life goals. But if we want to reach our goal, we have to train our ability to tolerate our uncomfortable inner experiences. Paradoxically, the best way to do this is to learn how to experience the uncomfortable inner experience more fully.

Emotional discomfort, not surprisingly, can be painful. When we experience emotional discomfort, we resist, judge, or run away from this feeling in hopes of avoiding the pain. We try to numb the discomfort, perhaps with a glass of wine or three. We may even hurt ourselves or engage in other kinds of self-harm. But by doing these things, we only make our situation worse. One of the great ways to overcome challenging emotions and thoughts is to develop mental resilience, and we can do this by staying positive. In this section, we'll learn how to develop mental resilience by positively managing a powerful emotion, "anger".

While well-managed anger can be a useful emotion that motivates you to make positive changes, uncontrolled anger can ruin your happiness, your mental health, and your life. In this section, we'll learn how to master anger skillfully.

One of the important aspects of mastering anger is learning how to deal with hurtful insults using positive humor. Every one of us is gifted with a sense of humor to some degree. But not many of us know how to use humor to release anger and be happier all around.

There is a story about Buddha that I like to keep in mind.

Once, Buddha and a large following of monks were passing through a village. Suddenly, a young man appeared and started throwing all sorts of mean insults at him. But Buddha remained unruffled by those insults. He politely requested that the young man come forward. Then he asked,

"If someone buys you a nice gift and you refuse to accept it, to whom does the gift belong?"

The young man answered that it would remain the property of the giver. "Exactly so," Buddha continued, "I refuse to accept your insults; does it not then still belong to you?"

So, if you find yourself on the receiving end of harsh criticism or a hurtful insult, instead of reacting angrily, use positive humor as your defense. But if your wit is not quick enough, avoid showing any response at all. Your non-response will rob them of their pleasure.

You can use positive humor to overcome any emotional discomfort and improve your mental resilience. When we learn to have a humorous perspective on life, even when faced with stressful events, we can transform even the most unbearable emotional pain into something bearable. In the next chapter, we're going to learn how to overcome the torrents of negative thoughts.

Chapter 11 - Navigating Roadblocks on the Road to Positivity

Overcoming the Torrent of Negativity

When we lose our belief in ourselves, we unwittingly sabotage our progress with negativities. We go through a daily torrent of negative thoughts, lose focus on our goals, and let fear, doubt, and confusion overshadow our hopes and dreams. To overcome the torrents of negativity, we not just have to break our negative habits but also the addictive behaviors that accompany them.

To change the negative thinking habits and addictive behaviors, first, we have to identify them. List the thinking habits and behaviors you want to change, which may include everything from black-and-white thinking and biting nails to jumping to conclusion thinking and overspending.

Now, pick an addictive behavior from your list, such as smoking or eating junk food. Now think about the situational and emotional context that triggers that behavior. Situations that trigger the craving for smoking or eating unhealthy foods can be negative thoughts or events that cause stress or boredom. Write down when you mostly feel the impulse to smoke or eat junk food. Write a few notes about how you feel and what you think when you experience the urge. Or you can maintain a thought diary. Here is the simple structure for a thought diary:

Column 1: Situation

Identify the moment when the craving surfaces. Did you feel stressed when you experienced the craving, or was there any other reason why the cravings occur?

Column 2: How do you feel?

Express your feelings in one word, like angry, sad, or frustrated.

Column 3: Negative thoughts

Identify the negative thoughts that bring forth the bad feeling or thoughts closely related to bad feelings (if the bad feeling triggers the urge to eat unhealthy or smoke)

Column 4: Rate your moods

In this final stage, go back to your moods in column 2 and re-rate them.

Where I am now	Emotion Or Feeling	Negative thought	My mood score

You'll also need to make some lifestyle changes to break free from addictive behaviors. Here are some areas of your life where you may need some change:

Availability: If the triggers of your negative behaviors are readily available, you may need to change your environment.

Activities: If you spend a considerable amount of time involved in that behavior, you may need to look for other ways to spend your time.

Relationships with peers: If the people you mix with contribute to maintaining your addictive behaviors, you may need to limit the time you spend with them.

Exercise: Identifying your triggers

Give a brief description of two thoughts or situations that triggered your negative behaviors

Trigger thought/ situation 1:...............................

Trigger thought/situation 2...................................

Now describe the normal consequences related to this thought or situation (both negative and positive consequences)

The negative consequence of trigger thought/ situation 1_____.

Negative consequences of trigger thought/ situation 2_____

The next step is to develop new choices for the trigger thoughts/situations you've described.

Describe two choices and their probable consequences for your first trigger thought/ situation. For each choice, briefly describe what would happen if you made that choice.

Possible consequences of choice 1:_____

Possible consequences of choice 2:_____

After describing the possible consequences, our task is to explain what needs to be done to obtain those choices. Therefore, briefly describe how you could put your choice into practice.

Choice 1: Change plans

Choice 2: Change plans.

Remember, changing old negative thinking habits and behaviors takes great commitment. If you don't see the problem, you won't have the mental strength to change your behavior. The more honest you are with yourself about the nature of your negative thinking habits or behaviors, the more likely it is that you'll take measures to break them.

Negative behavior takes years to develop. You can't just shake them off in an instant. Therefore, be patient and don't try to change too much at once. Start small and gradually increase until you get the desired result. Maintain a diary or journal to record your progress and keep yourself motivated. However, despite your best efforts, you may experience occasional relapses, which is quite normal. If it happens, find out why you slipped. Record the incident in your diary. You can carry around "coping cards" with you. These small cards may contain positive statements, motivational quotes, distraction techniques, breathing exercises, and other techniques. You can prevent relapse by gaining motivation by looking at the coping cards. However, if you experience relapses very often, you may need additional support.

Building Consistency in Positive Thinking

To keep feeling positive in life, we must commit to ourselves to choose positive thoughts. When you think of a positive thought, it creates a ripple effect that leads to positive inner dialogue, and ultimately, you'll start feeling good. More positive thoughts will result in more positive feelings. The goal is to consistently generate enough positive thoughts to create positive thought chains. In this way, we can develop consistency in positive thinking. And the best way to do it is by practicing gratitude.

For some of us, a gratitude practice can be a bit challenging to master because it takes a while to overcome the mental barriers that keep us from experiencing the positive feeling of gratitude.

But if you put aside 15 minutes per day, at least three times per week for at least three weeks, for doing a gratitude exercise, you'll find that expressing gratitude is becoming natural to you.

There are many ways to make gratitude a part of your day. But I recommend writing a gratitude journal. It is now five years on, and gratitude journaling has become a part of my life. Writing in a gratitude journal makes me feel elevated and more in control, and it also helps me bounce back from stress. Practicing gratitude makes me feel that my life is abundant now and that I already have all I need for this moment.

Gratitude journaling is extremely simple to start. You can use a journal or notebook for this purpose. If you don't enjoy writing on paper or are more comfortable with doing things digitally, you can use a gratitude app or even a simple Word document for tallying the good things.

Any time of the day is fine for journaling exercises. But the ideal time is the morning after you have your breakfast.

For practicing gratitude journaling, sit in a relaxed posture and allow your mind to calm down. Softly smile as you start your writing.

Now, remember things, persons, or events that give you peace. Take time to think. Remember the persons who made your life worthwhile. You can be thankful for your parents, children, siblings, best friends, lovers, or anyone who made your life meaningful and gave you peace. Write short sentences; don't bother with the grammar; it's the feeling that matters. If you have enough time to elaborate on why you feel grateful for having those things/ events/ people in your life, you can describe them briefly. Focusing on people for whom you're grateful has a greater impact than focusing on things for which you are grateful. However, it becomes equally effective if you become thankful to the universe or God for the things you receive in life.

You can also start by thanking the universe for your existence— for who you are, for all you have, and for the love that surrounds you.

Go for depth. Don't make a superficial list. If you elaborate in detail about someone or something for which you're grateful, it becomes more effective. For instance, writing "I'm grateful that my colleagues brought me food when I was sick on Wednesday" will be more effective than "I'm grateful for my colleagues." Therefore, make it clear why you're grateful for the items you add.

Savor every word. Gratitude journaling is not like another chore to get through. Bring up the feeling of thankfulness as you remember and write about someone or something. Don't rush.

Don't just add items to your list— reflect on what your life would be like without a certain person or a certain help, then express your heartfelt gratitude. Don't reluctantly journal because you think you should; don't practice with distaste.

There are innumerable things for which you might be thankful. You can be grateful for your health, your achievements, and your material possessions. You can even appreciate a beautiful flower in the garden or the sweet sounds of singing birds. You'll never run out of things to feel grateful for.

Don't set a minimum number of things to write in your journal every day. Some experts recommend five or so items per day. But in my experience, there are days when I have a lot to write and days I have less, and that's perfectly okay.

Be creative about journaling. Make it a pleasant activity.

Don't overdo it. Writing three days a week is more beneficial than writing every day.

Be patient. It will take a while to obtain the desired result. Commit to three weeks, and don't quit before then. The feeling of gratitude will arise spontaneously. Refrain from forcing the mind to generate that feeling. Just pretend, and after a few weeks of practice, the feeling will appear spontaneously.

Tackling Misunderstandings about Positive Thinking

There are lots of myths surrounding positive thinking. People think that it's about being in denial, pretending things are great even when they are not, or always putting on a fake smile. They say it's all about looking at a situation that might be not-so-great and finding some good in it, or, at the very least, surrendering defeat and accepting it the way it is.

But positive thinkers live healthier and longer than the rest. Don't believe it? The science says so!

A study performed in 2019 suggests that people with higher levels of optimism live 11–15% longer than those who are pessimistic. Now, doesn't that make you want to invite positivity into your life?

Here are some of the common myths:

Myth: When I'm a positive thinker, I must feel happy all the time.

Not at all. The positive thinker looks at the situation just the way it is. Then ask themselves, "Can I change it?", "If so, what can I do to change it?" If nothing can be done, the positive thinker makes his peace and moves on. So, it's more about contentment.

Myth: You can be positive with almost no effort.

Positivity is like a mental muscle. If you work out your muscles, they will become strong. Some people are naturally more positive than others. But to maintain a positive mindset, everyone needs to practice it either consciously or unconsciously. So, practice positive thinking like a new workout. Practice being thankful even for the trivial things, smile more often, and reward yourself even for the tiny accomplishment.

Myth: When I'm positive everything will turn out okay

Nope. You can't use positive thinking like magic to fix everything. You'll still need time and effort to work things out. Bad things may still happen. And when something bad happens, and you're a positive thinker, you'll look for creative ways to solve the problem.

Myth: No negative emotions, please!

Negative thoughts and emotions will inevitably arise. No matter how much you try, you can't stop negative thoughts from crossing your mind- that would be unrealistic and improbable. The aim of thinking positively is not suppressing negative thoughts or emotions but rather dealing with them better and more reasonably.

In the next chapter we're going to learn how to stay motivated during tough times.

Chapter Nine

Chapter 12 - Fueling Your Journey with Unwavering Motivation

Challenges to Motivation

Motivation is the energizing force that keeps you going. It is important to keep yourself continually motivated so that you stay positive and can keep on working enthusiastically toward your goal.

Accountability is a great motivator that will keep you on the right track. So, try to stay accountable. Match yourself with people who have similar goals, then form a group. You can commit yourself to this group. You may also read motivational books and watch motivational YouTube videos. It will give you a quick boost of inspiration. There are hundreds of motivational videos on YouTube. Also, watch acceptance speeches. Because watching someone at their best will make you feel excited and inspire you to succeed.

As you try your best to stay motivated in your positive thinking journey, there are challenges you have to keep in mind while chasing big financial goals.

If you're reluctant to get out of your comfort zone, you'll never reach your life goals. In order to expand beyond yourself, you have to expand your comfort zone. Climbing a flight of stairs is one way you can look at working toward a goal. Working on a big goal is a climb, an adventure— it is not for the faint heart. As a climber, you must make sure that you have the passion, the purpose, and the motivation to destroy your comfort zone and take risks.

If you don't have the courage to fail, sometimes publicly, even enormously, you will never attain your greatest goal. You'll need profound courage to face the potential of failure. Accepting failure as a possibility helps a person focus on success. The fear of failure will direct your attention toward failure. Therefore, don't let yourself be paralyzed by the fear of failure. Every successful person who lived in the trenches knew that failure leads to ultimate success.

- If you care about what others think, you'll never reach your biggest goal. You really don't need others' approval to succeed. Don't pay attention to the noise of the Coulds, Shoulds, and Woulds of external opinion. Instead, remain focused on your goal and keep moving forward. The irrational obsession about seeking others' approval will make you their prisoner. Successful individuals know how to turn down the volume of others' opinions and follow their own instincts.

They know the difference between approval and respect. They also know that we just can't please everyone in life. When they navigate the turbulent sea of life, they are not simply interested in winning any popularity contest.

• If you fail to convince yourself that you deserve to attain your life goal, you'll never reach your goal. If the condescending voice in your head tells you that you're never good enough, and you believe it, you'll never be successful. It is the voice of low self-esteem, which wants to keep you trapped in a life of low expectations and low rewards.

• The process of chasing a big goal is a game you should enjoy— a funny game with serious rules. Therefore, learn to gamify the process— learn to monitor your progress without the emotional and physical strain of worrying. Turn the process of planning into a game you love to enjoy so that it feels less like a chore and more like a hobby.

Stay true to yourself. Find out if you're chasing after a whim or if there is an inner compulsion. Compulsion is more powerful than mere desire. It is intense and persistent. You can ignore a desire, but you can't ignore a persistent craving, a fierce compulsion. This craving or compulsion is your greatest motivator. If you feel compelled, you're more likely to devote all your attention and strength to reach your goal. Even if you fall flat on your face repeatedly, you will always have the energy to pick yourself up and start all over again. Therefore, cultivate this compelling force within yourself to sustain your motivation throughout the pursuit of your goals.

When you have that motivation, you'll develop hyper-focus, discipline, and a persistent and devoted energy to see your vision come to fruition. Don't mistake a desire for compulsion. Only you can hear the growling of your inner giant. Only you can know if your vision will light up the often treacherous path of your life's journey. Inner compulsion or inner motivation is mandatory to reach your dream.

Staying Motivated During Hard Times

During difficult times, we often get overwhelmed and fearful. We lose our motivation, and our reactions are often anger and disappointment. Torrents of negative thoughts overwhelm us, and as we don't know how to stay strong in hard times, we suffer.

But the key is not to react but to respond logically. With the right mindset and motivation, we can manage our negative emotions and realign our thoughts to seek solutions. In this section, we will learn about the teachings of Stoic philosophers to stay motivated during tough times.

Epictetus suggested that we should approach life somewhat as if it were a game. We are like the people who play dice for fun, whose goal is to follow the rules and play fairly well in good spirits. They may win or lose, but in the end, it does not make any difference. However, they must accept whatever roll of the dice falls to them and try to make the best of it. Of course, they will try to win the game to become good players, but winning is not the ultimate goal— it's the "participation" that counts.

Some ancient Greek philosophers used the "reserve clause," an intelligent mental trick that allowed them to interact with the external world, people, and events without compromising the principle of "only choosing to do what is within their control." Whenever they planned to do something, they added a caveat like, "If nothing prevents me," "if fate permits," or "God willing," which helped them to accept the outcomes of their actions. Here are some examples:

"If nothing prevents me, I'll sail across the Atlantic to the Caribbean."

Or "If God willing, I'll become the next CEO of my company."

Or "If fate permits, I'll win a state championship."

These statements reflect the following attitude:

"I'll do what I must. Let things happen as they should. I can't rationally demand that my actions must produce the intended outcome, so I embark on my journey with an open mind, prepared to accept either success or failure with total equanimity".

The philosopher Antipater used the analogy of an archer shooting at a target to explain where it makes sense to focus your effort:

Imagine you're the archer, and you're aiming to hit the center of the bulls-eye of the target. Picture yourself notching the arrow and shooting as perfectly as possible.

Now, once the arrow leaves the bow, it is out of your control. You can only wait and see if it hits the target or not. You can't be certain how the wind will deflect the arrow from its path, nor whether your lack of skill will deviate the arrow, nor whether (for it is within the bounds of possibility) a bird will fly directly in front or whether your bow will break the moment you release the arrow. The only thing within your power is to shoot well.

Like an archer, you won't be disappointed if you fail to hit the bull's eye because you know that you did the most of it within your power.

When we plan our day ahead with the "reserve clause" in mind, we undertake any action with mindfulness and complete acceptance of the fact that the outcome may not turn out as intended. In this way, we become able to maintain our tranquility instead of getting frustrated if we don't get the expected results.

In his writing, Epictetus advised his students to withdraw their minds both from desires and aversion to external events. He also forbade terming them as good or bad and asked them to accept them unconditionally. So, let's devote our full attention to the task at hand and do our best to achieve success. And at the same time, keep in mind that the outcome is not wholly in our power, and we have to accept success and failure equally. We need to employ this approach throughout our lives.

Using a reserve clause while undertaking an action certainly helps us to accept the outcome of our actions. But in addition to using caveats "like fate permitting," it is important to prepare our minds for any outcome. If we adopt this mindset, we can stay motivated even during the hard times.

When we contemplate possible future adversity, we learn to take away the surprise or shock that accompanies it when it occurs in reality. We view them as something natural and don't feel distressed. This helps us maintain a positive outlook and continue with our lives, even when we're feeling down because of failures or tough times. In the next chapter, we're going to discuss how to foster an open mind.

Chapter Ten

Chapter 13 – Navigating the Sea of Skepticism

We all experience self-doubt; it's a natural part of life. Every one of us goes through times when we question our abilities, and for some of us, this tendency becomes so persistent that it shapes our lifestyle. While excessive confidence can lead to problems, losing all belief in our abilities is equally damaging. The question is: Can we break free from this tendency and regain our confidence? Or, at the very least, how can we improve our confidence level?

Before that, let's find out the root cause of your skepticism and self-doubt. The causes of self-skepticism can be multifactorial. That means it may not be caused by one thing but results from a combination of factors, including negative thinking and traumatic experiences. Let us discuss some of these factors:

The family home: One of the most powerful contributors to the development of self-skepticism can be the family environment. Our family affects our personality, behavior, and the way we see the world. Much of what we know about ourselves and how the world works, we learned from our family when we grew up. Our core beliefs about life start to form from early childhood, which are the strongest factors that influence our personality. These beliefs may include who and what we are, whether or not we can trust others, how much control we have over our lives, and whether other people and circumstances control our lives. We also start to know whether we are valuable or whether we deserve respect. We watch and listen to the people around us and learn all those basic principles.

Children can learn self-skepticism from parents if one or both parents lack confidence. Also, if a child grows up in a family environment where the following conditions are typical, they can also develop self-skepticism:

- There are lots of conflicts between the parents
- Parents are overly critical of their children. They seek perfection and blame themselves or their children when things are not right.

If you are a parent and find your child displaying low confidence and self-skepticism, take the necessary steps. Motivate them to take challenges, add fun activities to your family routine, and encourage them to participate in hobbies and other social and leisure pursuits.

Traumatic experiences: People may develop skepticism from experiences. We may not have a complete understanding of how self-confidence grows, but we do know that in many individuals, self-doubt is formed in childhood or adolescence and continues throughout life. A child who is teased or bullied because of being different may grow up as a person with low self-worth and develop self-doubt. For instance, if a child is teased for stuttering, he or she may gradually develop avoidance behavior that leads to self-skepticism.

Speech difficulty may disappear in time or thorough speech therapy treatment, but their attitude of skepticism may persist.

Although Bullying, harassment, and teasing within schools are not uncommon, some people can't forget the feeling of embarrassment, which continues to affect their level of self-confidence.

Unaddressed self-skepticism: If self-doubt or skepticism is left unaddressed in childhood, it may continue in adulthood. However, you may develop self-doubt at any point in your life. If you continually go through stressful life situations such as work stress, death in the family, or ongoing worry about finances, you may experience a decline in confidence. You can also develop skepticism if you constantly indulge in negative thinking and tend to use lots of negative words when thinking about yourself.

Being obsessive about perfection

Striving for quality is admirable, but if you take your perfectionist habit too far, it will lower your self-confidence and bring skepticism. People who are confident avoid the perfectionist's mind trap.

When you are caught in the trap of perfectionism, you feel horrible when you make a mistake. And that gives rise to self-doubt.

Comparing yourself to others

One of the biggest contributors to skepticism is the self-defeating habit of comparing ourselves to others and coming up short. While this tendency sometimes helps us to improve in the future, most people usually end up comparing their weaknesses against others' strengths. When we compare our worst to others' best, we set ourselves up for failure. People who are already struggling with a healthy perception of themselves will feel this comparison validates their sense of inadequacy, incompetence, and powerlessness.

The habit of comparing ourselves with others leaves us feeling driven to excel and often defeated. It deceives us into thinking that we lack the skill, talent, money, or looks.

If you find any of the above factors contributed to your self-skepticism, it's time to change some of your thinking habits, like comparing yourself to others and focusing too much on perfection.

Overcoming Skepticism

You may have already discovered the root causes of your self-skepticism and taken some steps to fix them. But your tendency to wallow in past mistakes will still foster self-doubt and diminish your confidence. Therefore, to beat self-skepticism, you must free yourself from the unhealthy habit of dwelling on mistakes.

Making mistakes may be unpleasant, but it is inevitable in everyone's life. None of us are perfect; we all make mistakes; it's written into our biology that we will make them. We learn from our mistakes. It's OK to make mistakes sometimes, and if you're lucky enough, the mistakes can be fixed. While mistakes can help you grow as a person, continually regretting your mistakes will deplete your self-esteem. Therefore, we have to recover from our mistakes and move on.

Stop dwelling on it!

If we had superpowers, we would undo every mistake we made in life. The feeling of defeat is awful. It drains your self-esteem and makes you feel like you're carrying a heavy burden on your shoulders. But if you are constantly obsessed with what happened and beat yourself up for your mistake, you're preparing yourself for more defeat. It is in your best interest to limit the damage from your mistakes and learn from them as much as possible. You have to get past your frustration and guilt to move forward.

After making a mistake, most of us fall into one of two camps: those with a skeptical mindset who think they will never be good at this, and those with a growth mindset who view that mistake as a "wake-up call." They figure out what went wrong and then adapt accordingly.

Research shows that the best way to learn from mistakes is to embrace the string of failure. Discover the benefits and lessons in your mistakes. The mistakes we make don't come with a log file or stack trace. But they surely come with lessons. Therefore, take a magnifying glass to your slop up and find out where things went wrong. Determine what exactly caused the error. You may realize there are patterns in your performance that contribute to that error. Once you identify the pattern, you can work on ways to fix it. Create a plan for how you'll avoid similar mistakes in the future. Don't lose the lessons.

Own your errors.

Accept your fault right away because ethical people don't hesitate to own up to their mistakes. After you've made a mistake, the worst thing you can do is attempt to sweep it under the rug and pretend that nothing happened. Don't always be a "quiet fixer."

Errors may often have side effects, and pretending that it did not happen can bring negative consequences. If anyone is affected by your mistake, make a real apology; don't make lame and self-protective statements. After apologies are made, your next step will be to find out whether you can do anything to remedy your fault. This may involve some extra work on your plate. But your apologies are pointless if you're not keen to accept the consequences.

Making mistakes is part of the process of becoming better. Remember, mistakes are there to guide you, not define you.

The final step of recovering from your mistake is to let go and move on. But it is not easy for many of us. Remember, being constantly obsessed over your failures and shortcomings won't do any good; it will rather prevent you from being productive and generate more failures. Do everything you can to recover from your mistake. And once you're done, smooth things up by taking a deep breath and moving on with a clear head. You don't want the "stomach in our shoes" feeling when you know that you've made a big mistake. It does not matter how bad you feel about your fault; what matters is how you bounce back from it.

Fostering an Open Mind

The reality is that both skepticism and self-doubts are states of mind. Overcoming skepticism takes some time and effort. You can't just turn from a skeptic to a confident person overnight. It is a gradual process. But if you're willing to put in some hard work and dedication and stick to your practice, you'll soon notice positive results. Nurturing an open mind wipes away self-doubts and skepticism. It becomes possible when developing an awareness of feelings.

Feelings allow us to know ourselves. In our day-to-day lives, we go through various feelings—self-doubt is also a feeling.

Generally, we can classify feelings into three types: pleasant, unpleasant, and neutral.

If you don't notice your feelings, you may find the third type of feeling a little confusing. The neutral feeling can't be identified as pleasant or unpleasant. If you feel numb, it is a neutral feeling. If you experience a mixed emotion, which feels neither good nor bad, it is also neutral.

As you focus on your feelings, you can quickly identify them as favorable, unfavorable, or neutral. Because when you are experiencing a favorable feeling, no unwanted or neutral feeling is there. The same is true for unfavorable and neutral feelings. You can't experience multiple emotions or sensations at once. When you become aware of the movements of feelings, you realize that feelings are constantly changing without your conscious control.

Say, for example, that you are in a good mood now. It's a sunny day; you've just finished your work and are heading home, thinking about a good dinner. Although, unconsciously, you are clinging to that happiness, after a while, you will discover that you are no longer feeling the joy. It has faded away, and now you are feeling neutral. Then, perhaps you recall an argument with a colleague at work, and your neutral feeling changes to an unpleasant feeling.

As you notice these changes in feelings, you understand that feelings are short-lived. Now, whenever the feeling of self-doubt enters your mind, become aware of it.

Also, become aware of the emotions that come with self-doubt. Identify those emotions, and give yourself permission to recognize and accept them. Look at them without judgment. Allow them to flow without the slightest interruption. Neither encourage them nor discourage them. Simply observe as they appear, peak, and disappear. Developing awareness of your feelings and emotions will help you let go of the attitude of skepticism that holds you back. In the next chapter, we're going to learn how to overcome the challenge of staying positive.

Chapter Eleven

Chapter 14 - Planting Positivity: Cultivating the Habit of Positive Thinking

Consistency: The Key to Positive Thinking

Our long-standing thought patterns took ages to develop, and despite our best efforts, we can't change them overnight. So, if you fail to notice any improvement in a day or two, don't be hard on yourself. Improving thought patterns requires patience and consistent effort. Training your mind is similar to learning a physical skill; it'll involve some trial and error, and you'll make slow progress in the beginning. However, the more consistent you are with your practice, the better you'll become. Even if you struggle to shift your thoughts, the act of trying is itself a big step. Because when you try, you build awareness and control over your cognitive processes.

Remember, our goal is not to stop the negative thoughts from forming altogether but to manage them effectively so that they don't dominate our mindset and dictate our actions. When we learn to consistently focus on the positive aspects of life, our thoughts will naturally shift to a more positive and constructive pattern.

Overcoming the Biggest Challenge to Staying Positive

The most challenging part of developing a positive mindset is overcoming the negative forces in our minds. You already know that dealing with negative thoughts is one of the major struggles you might encounter while rewiring your brain for positivity. But the self-blaming negative thoughts, which we term the "inner critic," are a powerful internal enemy that will try to rob you of your confidence and disconnect you from your inherent power through destructive criticism. This critical inner voice can affect all aspects of your life by fostering limiting beliefs and emotional wounds you've picked up in a lifetime. Taming the inner critic is very critical for eliminating negativity.

The voice of the inner critic resembles that of our parents or primary caregivers. If you pay attention to the voice in your head that tells you that you are worthless, you'll find that it's the voice of either your parents or a parental figure. This critical inner voice is actually our early life experiences that are internalized or taken in as ways we view ourselves and the world. This voice sets impossible standards of perfection and beats you up for the smallest mistakes. It wants you to believe that you are weak and that reaching your goal is impossible.

Identify your inner critic and hear what this voice has to say. While recognizing the self-critic, remind yourself that this negative voice is not a reflection of your reality. Remind yourself that you are an infinite being and that your potential is limitless.

Write the inner critic's statements in the second person. For instance, a statement like, "I'm wasting my time. I'm such a fool," should be written as "You are wasting your time. You're such a fool". This will help you see your thoughts from a different perspective and help you understand that these statements are not true. Then, respond to the thought by writing down a more realistic, constructive, and positive statement.

In response to a thought like, "You're wasting your time," you could write a positive and compassionate statement like, "I'm utilizing the time by learning something new, and I'm enjoying it." If you don't enjoy the thought-replacement writing, repeat it in your mind. The purpose of this thought replacement is to develop a more honest attitude toward yourself.

The inner voice will get louder as you make progress. It will try to hold you back. Use the thought replacement technique when this voice tries to put you down.

The next step is to keep company with positive People. To stay mentally sound, it is important that you surround yourself with people who inspire you, encourage you, and help you realize your potential. While it is quite difficult, even impossible, to get rid of negative thoughts, we can choose to spot and weed out toxic people from our lives.

With their bad attitudes, catastrophic thinking, and fatalistic outlooks, those toxic people can drain your mental energy and your self-esteem. They will not just discourage you from taking on challenges but also drag you down with them to the dark side.

Do you know people who constantly complain about their lives? They may have legitimate problems, but they seem to enjoy wallowing in their misery instead of trying to work their way through obstacles. They can be your acquaintances, friends, neighbors, or co-workers. You have to choose not to listen to those people.

While positive people can boost your mood and raise your vibration, negative people do the opposite—they tend to be an energy drain. They will suck the positive energy out of you to fuel their negativity and leave you emotionally drained and depressed.

Many times, we unwittingly give those negative individuals influence over our thoughts, behaviors, and feelings. These people are great at discouraging you and giving you negative feedback. If you hang around with them and listen to them long enough, you'll start to feel that you're having negative self-talk. So, weed out these negative people from your life. If you can't detach them completely, limit the amount of time you spend with them. And include more people in your network who seem balanced, positive, and wise.

Use a Mindful approach to Cultivate Positive Thinking.

Mindfulness is a wonderful tool to cultivate positive thinking. Do you mindfully ease into the morning with some positive thinking, a healthy meal, exercise, and activities? It is important because what you do in the morning determines whether you succeed or fail throughout the rest of the day. I always emphasize positively starting my morning, because a good morning ritual leaves a powerful ripple effect on my mood, happiness, and sense of self-worth. Highly successful individuals craft their morning rituals to maximize their energy, productivity, and creativity all day long. Don't start your morning in a rushed panic. The Greek philosopher Seneca would start his day by rehearsing his plans for the day. He would prepare himself for the things that could go wrong. According to Seneca, *"Nothing happens to the wise man against his expectation... nor do all things turn out for him as he wished but as he reckoned—and above all, he reckoned that something could block his plans."*

Become mindful of your decisions. When you become mindful, you become more aware of the various factors that influence your decision-making. And this awareness leads to less subjectivity in the decision-making process. To make mindful decisions, here are the steps to follow:

1. Before making a decision, spend a few seconds centering yourself in the present moment. Pay attention to the process of your breathing.

2. Softly close your eyes and sit with the question. Hold the question in your mind, but avoid the temptation to seek the answer. Just keep repeating the question in your head.

3. Now, explore the question with kindness and curiosity.

4. Open your eyes and analyze all the information you have. Now you're ready to make informed and unbiased decisions.

Become more mindful of your communication. Mindful communication is about being fully present with others, listening with an open, non-judgmental heart to your colleagues, and responding effectively. In this busy world of the modern-day workplace, much of our communication is done without proper listening and jumping to decision-making even before fully understanding the issue or problem. Being mindful during communication allows us to get to the nub of the issue more quickly, and saves time, effort, and frustration for all concerned. Here are four steps I recommend you follow while communicating mindfully at your workplace:

1. Connect. Learn to look through the eyes of others. Pay mindful attention to what the other person is saying in this moment and ask for clarification if necessary.

2. Agree. Look for things to agree on.

3. Collaborate. Work with your colleagues as equals to find a solution for the issue at hand.

4. Achieve. Work together on the solution and attain the work goal.

Learning to stay mindful will not just help you stay positive but also let go of the thoughts and emotions that don't serve you. In the next chapter, we will discover how to embrace a positive future.

Chapter 15 - Embracing Your Future with Positivity

The Long-Term Benefits of Positivity

In the previous chapters, we discussed the health benefits of positive thinking; in this section, let's learn about some of the long-term cognitive benefits of positivity:

Positivity makes you a better problem solver. When you're a positive person, you remain calm and composed when you make decisions. That makes you better at problem-solving. As a positive thinker, you believe in yourself and think the results will be favorable.

Positivity makes you feel more energetic.

Several studies have shown that positive thinkers feel more energetic than negative thinkers. A positive outlook keeps stress at bay and makes people happy and active at all times.

When you're in a good mood, your brain releases happy hormones called endorphins. This hormone raises your energy level and motivates you to take on challenges.

According to one study published in Forbes, people who are generally happy, are more energetic and productive than sad people.

The researchers found that employees who are content with life are 180% more energized than their less content counterparts, 150% more satisfied with life, and 155% more content with their jobs. They feel 50% more motivated than the rest, which makes them 108% more engaged. As a result, they are 50% more productive than their colleagues, who have a negative view of life.

The research also revealed that happy workers spend 80% of their time during the week doing work-related tasks, while unhappy workers spend 40% of their time doing what they're there to do.

This means happy workers are twice as productive as unhappy workers.

Positivity opens your mind.

When you are a positive thinker, you become more open to new experiences and learning new skills. This contributes to your personal growth. A positive person is always ready to try new things, whether that means engaging in a new workout routine like dance fitness, learning a new craft hobby like pottery, or trying out fresh food like sushi; Positivity will give you the mental energy to experience something new.

Life-long Learning and Adaptability in Positive Thinking

Most of us associate learning with the teachings we receive from educational institutions. We are told from childhood to get a "good education."

It's true that the qualifications we receive from formal education are important in many ways. It helps us get better jobs, earn more money, and become financially successful.

However, formal education is just one type of learning opportunity among many to improve our knowledge and develop essential life skills.

You can obtain knowledge and gain new skills from anywhere- the process of learning is always happening, whether you're aware of it or not.

However, for lifelong learning, you have to develop a positive attitude to consciously learn to improve both your personal and professional lives. When you master this skill, it will enhance your understanding of the world and give you more opportunities to live your dream.

Lifelong learning will radically change your worldview and boost your confidence and self-esteem. It'll motivate you to challenge your old ideas and beliefs and take calculated risks. It will also make you more adaptable to change when it happens. Besides, the learning process will give you a rewarding experience because you don't have to learn for a specific reason.

It is thought that life-long learning promotes an active mind that can delay or even halt the progress of neurodegenerative diseases like dementia. Although there is not enough scientific evidence to support this claim, having an active mind does have other benefits since it will encourage you to learn more, which will give you a sense of fulfillment at any age. There are several stages of lifelong learning.

Motivation

Self-motivation is paramount for lifelong learning. You'll need a positive mindset toward learning and to feel positive about your ability to learn. If you don't have motivation, you'll fail to see the point of learning. Therefore, use the techniques you've learned in this book to motivate yourself.

Acquire

In this stage, you'll need to acquire information through reading, listening, and observing. Then, you'll practice what you've learned, experiment with the ideas, and learn from experience. Information is all around you: you'll only pick the ones that are relevant and meaningful and incorporate them into your skills.

Search

Learning becomes more effective when we can find meaning in the information we have gathered. We can easily remember information when we can understand it and become able to put it into context. Lifelong learning is about applying the knowledge you've gathered and asking yourself questions like: "How can this information or idea be helpful to make my life better?" or, "What has this experience taught me about life?"

Trigger

We humans are not very good at retaining information. No matter how hard you try, you'll never be able to remember all that you read, hear, and experience. But you can use various means to trigger your recollection, such as taking notes, experimenting with your skills, and discussing your ideas. In this way, you can learn and grow.

Examine

After gathering the information and experimenting with the ideas, make sure to regularly examine your knowledge. It will help you reinforce what you've learned. Keep an open mind so that you can question your understanding and remain open to new ideas. Talking to others and learning about their point of view can help you in this process.

Reflect

The final stage is reflecting on what you've learned. Spend some quiet time thinking about what you've learned and what motivated you to learn it. Ask yourself how this knowledge has benefited you and what you've learned from your mistakes. Remain positive as you reflect on your understanding.

Here is a stoic self-reflection exercise to help you stay positive.

Set a fixed time in the evening to do this exercise—not the time when you feel tired and in need of sleep. Aim for 5 to 10 minutes of uninterrupted time. Remove distractions—it is important to have all of your attention in the process. Clear your mind about the tasks you have to do tomorrow and allow your thoughts to become very quiet.

Now open your notebook, grab your pen, and ask yourself these three Pythagorean questions that Epictetus asked himself every day.

Question one: What did I do wrong?

(Did you allow yourself to be ruled by irrational fear or unhealthy desire? Did you sacrifice your balance and your peace and engage in activities that promote negativity?

(Did you act according to your reason or according to outward allurement?)

Question two: What did I do (right)?

(Did you act "appropriately" according to your authentic values and principles?)

Question three: What duty is left undone?

Did you fail to perform any of your duties diligently? (Did you omit any part of your duty?)

While reviewing the events of the day, picture them in your mind as vividly as possible. Appreciate yourself for all the good things you've done.

Now ask yourself the following two questions:

1. What bad habit of mine have I cured today?
2. In what respect am I better than I was yesterday?

Be 100% honest with yourself while answering these questions. Ask yourself more self-reflection questions if you like. Here are some examples:

- What could I have done better?
- What was the most important thing I did today?
- What am I grateful for today?
- What did I learn today?

You can add more questions if you like. But make sure not to overdo it. Reflecting on 4-5 questions should be enough. Focus on doing the self-reflection exercise at the same time every evening. Let a feeling of self-love and compassion arise as you practice.

If you don't enjoy writing, you can sit down and have a conversation with yourself in the form of questions and answers.

A Powerful Method for Continued Growth in Positive Thinking

In this section, you'll practice a thought experiment that will help maintain your growth in positive thinking. You're going to visualize your "self-ideal" to become the person we all desire to become.

Your ideal self is the image of an idealized individual you always wanted to be. They are the perfect person who sets the course for their life, has achieved whatever they want, and has gained complete peace of mind. We always measure ourselves against this model, and over time, these qualities start to form a vision of the person we hope to become.

The following exercise is based on the principle, "You become what you meditate on."

For this thought experiment, you'll need a quiet place. Sit comfortably. Now imagine how your ideal person spends their day.

They wake up in the morning, relaxed and invigorated. They do not appear to have any worries about the day ahead. They are always confident and prepared to meet every challenge with wisdom, prudence, and temperance. They don't react to other people's negativities but rather calmly address their concerns. When they work, they give their full and undivided attention to the task at hand. They are not envious of others. They can forgive others quickly and do not brood over things that are over. They are free from lust, anger, greed, attachment, and ego. They do not care if they have or do not. They are fully happy and content with their current life, regardless of their current circumstances.

To this description, you may add any quality that you think your ideal person should possess.

Now imagine yourself acting like this person. Imagine yourself dealing with the day ahead as this positive, calm, and peaceful person. Imagine yourself handling life's challenges with grace and calm and making it look effortless. Spend a while envisioning yourself as your "self-ideal" before ending this exercise.

Conclusion

We've come to the end of our journey together. You've learned the fifteen powerful steps to unleashing your inner greatness. The tried and tested methods you've learned in each stage will transform you into a positive person who believes they have complete faith in themselves to handle any and every challenge that comes their way in reaching their goals. Remember, you have the inner power to transform yourself at any given moment. So, start the journey to take your life to new heights of richness. Believe in yourself and take action— use what you have right now...Just start right now.

So, are you ready to chase your dream? Well, you will never, if you wait for the perfect time. There is no perfect moment yet to come, but you have the power to make this very moment "perfect." Your brain may trick you into believing it's not the right time or that you're not completely ready. But trust me—you'll never be ready. No one is ever ready to push through their fear and embrace the greatest changes. No one is ever ready to make the impossible possible.

If you choose to wait until all the problems are gone, and the conditions become perfect, you'll wait forever. There will always be problems and less-than-perfect conditions.

So don't stare at the ocean and hope it will ever rest—throw caution to the winds and set sail for the uncharted waters. There will be times of turbulence and moments of stillness— sometimes, you'll sail with the wind, sometimes against it. If you lay at anchor, how would you learn to sail in high winds and cross the ocean?

You have the inner power to transform yourself at any given moment. So, start the journey to take your life to new heights of richness. Believe in yourself and take action— use what you have right now. Just jump right now. I hope you'll put into practice what you've learned in this book.

Made in the USA
Columbia, SC
26 May 2024